OUTRAGEOUS GRACE

A Story of Tragedy and Forgiveness

Outrageous Grace

A Story of Tragedy and Forgiveness

Grace L. Fabian
Psa. 94:18

Grace Fabian

Ambassador International

GREENVILLE, SOUTH CAROLINA & BELFAST, NORTHERN IRELAND

www.ambassador-international.com

OUTRAGEOUS GRACE
A Story of Tragedy and Forgiveness

Printed in the United States of America

ISBN: 978-1-935507-08-6

First Edition—November, 2009
Second Edition—February, 2010
Third Edition—January, 2011

Cover Design & Page Layout by David Siglin of A&E Media

AMBASSADOR INTERNATIONAL
Emerald House
427 Wade Hampton Blvd.
Greenville, SC 29609, USA
www.ambassador-international.com

AMBASSADOR BOOKS
The Mount
2 Woodstock Link
Belfast, BT6 8DD, Northern Ireland, UK
www.ambassador-international.com

The colophon is a trademark of Ambassador

Dedication

My best cheerleaders, and the ones who have lived through this story with me, are my wonderful children. They did not translate a single word of the Nabak New Testament but they played a big part in it. They wanted me to finish it even after their father's death.

They used their experiences of being third-culture kids and became more adventuresome, more global than their peers. They have more flexibility in their little fingers than most people have in their whole body.

They asked for copies of all the stories they had seen me write over the years. That was when the idea for a book was born. They encouraged me to write it. I dedicate this book to them—

Jonathan,
Dietlinde,
Heidi,
Kurt.

What an awesome privilege to raise four Christian children and then share them with the world.

Endorsements

This is more than a dramatic account of the brutal murder of missionary Edmund Fabian in Papua New Guinea in 1993. Rather, it is the account of decades of challenging work to bring the Bible to the Nabak people of that island, providing a host of details that bring to life the joys and challenges of Bible translation amongst people whose language has never been reduced to writing. Yet the story does turn, in many ways, on the murder of Edmund and the choices his widow Grace made in the ensuing months and years. Thus it becomes an account of the outworking of the gospel itself: forgiveness, faithfulness, joy in the midst of suffering, and the sheer triumph of God's outrageous grace.

— **D. A. Carson**, Research Professor at Trinity Evangelical Divinity School, award winning author of over fifty books including *The Gagging of God*, founding chair of GRAMCORD.

I was spellbound reading Grace Fabian's story of her husband's murder and the redemption God wrought through this tragedy. One thing impresses me above all else. Grace and her family are anything but shallow Christians given to sensationalism. Instead, they are obviously firmly rooted in the soil of Scripture and recognize that God is sovereign over all things, including the temptations of our adversary. In the cauldron of her suffering, Grace has come to know ever more fully that nothing can befall us without first passing through the filter of God's love.

— **Hank Hanegraaff**, president of the Christian Research Institute and host of the *Bible Answer Man* Broadcast

Grace Fabian uses words and emotions like a vast array of vibrant colors and paints on the pages of her book the most vivid pictures of God at work in the midst of violent murder and unspeakable reconciliation. You will laugh, you will cry and you will praise God for His outrageous grace.
— **Russ Hersman**, Senior Vice President, Wycliffe Bible Translators

Try to put this book down! I couldn't. My friend Grace Fabian has given us a ponderous, convicting, inspiring, energizing, deepening look into her life. She has been transparent about how God gave her daily light when in the darkest experiences, courage in the fearful times and a willing heart—no matter what. Grace mentors us in what it looks like to be triumphant in the midst of ongoing heartache. Her willingness to walk toward, forgive and serve one whose actions resulted in great pain and loss has marked me forever. You won't read a book quite like this again.
— **Gail MacDonald**, author of many books including *High Call, High Privilege* and *Keep Climbing*

Enthralled, awed, and teary-eyed throughout, I have just finished reading your manuscript and could not stop until I'd read it all. I have no words to describe how grateful I am to our gracious heavenly Father for you and your unfathomable sacrifice for His people. We receive more manuscripts than we can actually read. In my more than fifteen years of working with the Christian Research Insitute, however, I've never read a manuscript that more bears the mark of Christ and is more worthy of promotion for the sake of His kingdom than your story.
— **Stephen Ross**, Christian Research Institute

Grace and Edmund Fabian were Wycliffe Bible translators working among the Nabak people of Papua New Guinea. Then, as they were nearing the completion of the Nabak New Testament, an astonishing and crushing tragedy struck them. In this book, Grace tells the story of that tragedy, and how God's astounding grace overcame the effects of that tragedy and transformed the lives of many people. Grace has written a remarkable and powerful book, filled with spiritual truths and deep insights. Hers is one of the most challenging and inspiring missionary stories I have ever read. I can whole-heartedly recommend this book.
— **Thomas Hale**, missionary doctor and author of many books including *Don't Let the Goats Eat the Loquat Trees* and *The Far Side of Liglig Mountain*

I thank God that I had the honor of being one of the people who helped Grace check the final books of the New Testament. I rejoice with her over God's mercy, love and provision in going the last mile to finish the work of Bible translation for the Nabak people. Her story is startling and honest and deserves a place with the great missionaries testimonies of our time.

— **Neil W. Anderson**, author of *In Search of the Source*, international speaker, former Bible translator, pastor.

I've known Grace and Edmund Fabian since their early years as missionaries in Papua New Guinea. But it was not until the shock of Edmund's murder that I began to really know Grace through her letters. Her honest faith poured through the bare elegance of her words. Now captured in this book, Grace's stories bring tears of compassion and joy, and a sense of wonder at the tenderness of God's greater plan. This is a must read, a powerful story needing to be told.

— **Virelle Kidder**, conference speaker and author of six books, including *Meet Me at the Well* and *The Best Life Ain't Easy*.

Fabian's tale of murder, persecution, forgiveness and victory is unforgettable. She describes God's "outrageous" grace and well earns a name for herself, Amazing Grace.

— **Carol Lee Anderson**, author of *Do You Know What You Are Doing, Lord?*, speaker, former Bible translator.

Acknowledgements

When I was five years old, my daddy used to pick me up and set me on the cross bar of his bicycle. I sat with my legs to one side and grabbed the handlebars. I loved the wind blowing through my hair as he pedaled. When we arrived at the church or the store, he would gently take me off, straighten my dress and take my hand.

My life has always been filled with people willing to give me a lift up, sit beside me, dust me off and take my hand. I am grateful for the people God placed in my life at strategic crossroads.

My parents gave me a godly heritage and burned into me a desire to know and cherish God's Word.

Bryan Burtch, you knew of my desire to be a missionary and suggested I go to linguistics school. You told me to think about serving with Wycliffe Bible Translators. I did.

One of the selling points of Wycliffe Bible Translators is the on-the-job training and the expertise of others who come alongside to help in the humongous task of Bible translation. Ken McElhanon surveyed languages on the Huon Peninsula and gave us a word list and insights into the Nabak grammar that moved us along in our quest to learn Nabak. Specialists like Joy Lloyd, Bruce Waters, Cindy Farr, Lillian Fleischman, Carl Whitehead and others, provided invaluable linguistic help. Twenty-two different Wycliffe consultants checked the books of the New Testament for accuracy as we completed them. It was only because of these people's invaluable insights and the way they pedaled behind us that enabled us to complete the task. Thank you .

So we could stay at the job over the years, many people have supported this work with finances, applause, care packages, letters, counsel, hospitality, love and prayers. God's Word in Nabak would never have happened without you giving us a lift up, and gentle care. I think there should be a 50-year plaque for you as well. Thank you for investing in Christ's kingdom purposes.

Thanks to my sisters, Kathryn, Carmilla and Mary. You are my greatest fans for saving all my letters and then giving them back to me when I told you I was writing a book.

My love to you, Jonathan and Amy, for going to P.N.G. and bringing a significant episode to the story. And thanks for giving me six grandchildren, whom I love to pieces.

Special thanks to you, Dietlinde, for your skillful help with the computer tasks related to this book, especially planning the family's final read-through. Matthew, you found one amazing gal.

The twins, Heidi and Kurt, you add another wonderful dimension to my world.

Thank you to you, Les Stobbe, my literary agent who has stood with me watching in wonder at how God put all of this together.

And God—My deep gratitude for Your amazing kindness to me and my family.

Table of Contents

Map of Papua New Guinea with key locations arrowed.

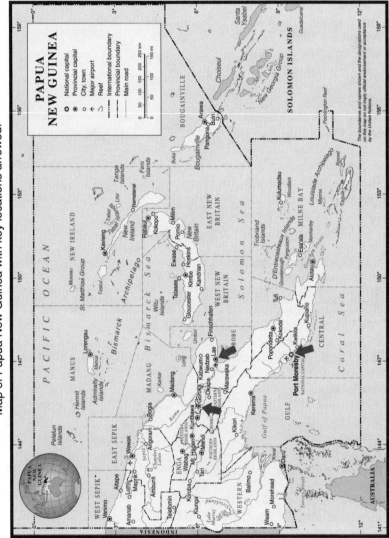

Foreword

When Christ calls a man, he bids him come and die.[1]

All four Gospels relate that Jesus, after rising from the dead, told his followers to go and take the Good News of salvation to everyone everywhere. Each Gospel gives its own flavor to the Great Commission but John's account is unique in that it illustrates the verbal command by including a visual message.

After he said this, he showed them his hands and side. The disciples were overjoyed when they saw the Lord. Again Jesus said, "Peace be with you! As the Father has sent me, I am sending you" (John 20:20-21).

It must have been startling for the disciples to realize that even in his glorified and resurrected body, Jesus retained the scars of his crucifixion. God the Father wanted those wounds to remain visible in the exalted body of his Son. Far from being a source of embarrassment or shame, those scars spoke more eloquently than words ever could of the reality of God's love and our redemption!

But there's more. Perhaps the most startling aspect of John's account is what Jesus said next. Even as he was showing them his hands and side he was commanding them to go into all the world. *As the Father has sent me, I am sending you.* They were looking at the scars at the very moment they were receiving the Great Commission. It was impossible for the disciples to misunderstand. The Father had sent the Son to lay down his life for others. He died so that others might live. And now the Son is sending his disciples into

[1] Bonhoeffer, Dietrich. *The Cost of Discipleship.* New York: Simon & Schuster, 1995: 89.

the world to do the same thing. The cross was to define not only the message they preached but the very way they lived their lives, in self-giving love for others. Paul understood this well.

We always carry around in our body the death of Jesus, so that the life of Jesus may also be revealed in our body. For we who are alive are always being given over to death for Jesus' sake, so that his life may be revealed in our mortal body. So then, death is at work in us, but life is at work in you (II Cor. 4:7-12).

Little wonder that the Greek word for "witness" (*martur*) soon came to describe those who literally gave their lives for the faith (martyr). To be a witness for Christ is by definition to be ready to give up one's life. But that is not a bad thing because losing one's life for Christ is the only way to find it (Luke 9:24)!

This book, *Outrageous Grace,* tells the story of Edmund and Grace Fabian, witnesses for Christ in the full meaning of that term. They found their lives by losing them. Not only that, because they allowed death to be at work in them, life was able to be at work in the Nabak people...and beyond!

As pastor of a church that has supported Fabians in their ministry since 1964, it is a joy to write the foreword for this book. Grace was the first missionary our church ever supported back when she started in Mexico. If you are like me, once you start reading, you'll find the narrative gripping and be unable to put it down. But more, you will find your heart deeply stirred as you laugh and weep with real people who simply allowed Jesus to send them into the world even as the Father had sent him into the world...to give his life so that others might find theirs.

The real question is: Who will go next? Who will be the witnesses (martyrs) for the generation to come? May every reader respond with a humble "Here am I, send me!"

— Pastor Stan Key
Loudonville Community Church
Fall 2009

❄ CHAPTER ONE

The birds keep singing

"My world stopped
in earth-shattering suddenness,
yet not one bird
stopped singing."[2]

A white-collared kingfisher swooped down, landing on a branch of the pine tree just outside my office window. Its azure blue feathers contrasted with the brilliant purplish-red color of the bougainvillea. That thorny vine draped itself around the pine branches like strings of Christmas tree lights. "Is there really a pine tree under there?" a friend had once asked.

Many unusual creatures like kangaroos, leatherback turtles and flashlight fish live on this island of Papua New Guinea connecting the Indian and Pacific Oceans.

I favored the exotic birds. I called them "feathered friends," mainly because they kept the insect population down, though they did more than minimize my chances of contracting malaria. There was something reassuring about their throaty notes and the way they glided through the air. They inserted an element of pleasure and peace into my high-energy schedule by their glorious songs and brilliant plumage.

I gave myself a little pat on the shoulder, proud that I could name so many of the birds of our adopted country—the man-

---
[2] Jones, Doris Moreland. *And Not One Bird Stopped Singing.* Nashville: Upper Room, 1997: 27.

nekin, lorikeet, honeyeater and lovely snow-white cockatoo. When my husband, Edmund, our children and I traveled back to America for what we missionaries call "furlough," I enjoyed telling people that Papua New Guinea has the largest pigeon in the world, the largest and tiniest parrots in the world, with at least eight hundred species of birds, more than the U.S. and Canada combined.

The kingfisher was a frequent visitor to this spot and my family laughed when they heard me greet him with a cheery, "Good afternoon, friend."

I kept my eyes on the kingfisher. This afternoon he seemed to be looking straight at me, like he knew something I didn't.

I felt a soft afternoon breeze through the open louver windows and reminded myself that at sunset, when vandals roam freely, we should remember to shut and lock all the windows. But now with the tropical sun's rays all around us, and friends beside us, we were safe, weren't we?

After a series of high-pitched nasal notes, as if in gentle warning, the kingfisher flew off. All I saw was a flash of blue wings. *I need to tend to the job at hand and stop the bird watching.* I smelled the coffee perking in the kitchen and glanced at the clock. We believed in coffee breaks almost as strongly as we believed in the work we had come to do on this fascinating island. We were missionary-translators, determined to learn the Nabak language, devise an alphabet, and eventually translate the Bible for this group numbering 25,000.

It was three o'clock in the afternoon. The steaming cups of coffee and plate of crackers and peanut butter I planned for my husband, the two Nabak translation helpers and myself, would give each of us a much needed boost of caffeine, sugar and protein for our translation work.

But then the older of the men ran past my window and out the driveway.

"Geŋ zigok?" I shouted. [3]

No answer.

"Where's Miliŋnâŋe going?" I called out, turning to my husband's office.

No answer.

Strange. I swiveled in my chair and walked through the tiny room adjoining our offices and peered into his office. If no one was around I'd wait with the coffee until they came back.

Instead of two men engaged in energetic discussion of Nabak words and phrases, my husband, Edmund, was alone at his computer, slumped back in his chair. An axe hung from the back of his head.

An axe? I stared. *Am I going mad? Surely I'm hallucinating.* Cold fear crept through my entire body.

"No, no, please, this can't be happening," I sobbed.

One minute my mind spun out of control, the next, I stood stupefied, refusing to believe the dreadful reality before me.

I rubbed my eyes, patted Edmund's shoulders and sensed the truth instantly. This was no dream. My teeth chattered. My stomach lurched.

Someone had murdered Edmund.

---

[3] The n with a tail is our way of writing the sound ng as in the English word 'sing'. The problem with writing it ng in Nabak is that this sound comes at the beginning and middle of words. It is a very frequent phoneme so it makes words twice as long. It is really one sound, a velar nasal, and needs one symbol. The other problem with using ng is that there are many words in Nabak where g follows the n sound, two sounds. For example 'nin-gat'.

Edmund and Grace Fabian. The last picture taken of Edmund before he died.

Photo by Pat Brien

❧ CHAPTER TWO
The terms

*"The Master Creator, unimaginably, wants to partner
with little me in redeeming His world—
but only on His terms,
terms that quite often are different from mine."*[4]

On the screen of my mind all of our successes in winning the hearts of the Nabak people, the struggles to master their language, the misery of dengue fever, being separated from two of our children, and the isolation, flickered past and seemed to explode in some kind of horror movie. Had it all come down to this?

A surge of adrenaline took over. Without hesitation, I pulled the axe out. Blood splattered everywhere—on my skirt, on the carpet, down Edmund's back. My hands were covered with blood—my husband's blood. *This is a sacred place, a room where we sing praise to God and pray every morning, dedicating ourselves to the holy task of Bible translation. This is not the way it's supposed to be.*

I dropped the axe on the floor and ran to the phone to call for help. "Someone has just killed my husband," I stammered. My voice didn't even sound like it belonged to me.

Then I raced back to the office. It was far too late for any first-aid treatment I could give but I tried pressing the gaping wound together anyway. I stepped back from that hideous sight.

---

[4] O'Donnell, James. *Letters for Lizzie.* Chicago: Northfield, 2004: 200.

Could this be the same Thursday that started with me humming while I scrambled the eggs for breakfast?

That very morning I had brimmed with excitement over the idea of finishing our missionary project, the translation of the Nabak New Testament. What a beautiful Thursday on the tropical island of Papua New Guinea! Just yesterday, Edmund and I had finished the major check of the Gospel of Luke: a milestone. And he had only four more chapters to go in I Corinthians.

"God's in His heaven and all's right with the Fabian world," I declared as he and our 16-year-old twins, Heidi and Kurt, joined me for breakfast. Daughter Heidi gave thanks for the food and prayed for her big brother, Jonathan, and big sister, Dietlinde, back in the United States.

As everyone paid attention to their fruit juice and toast, I announced, "We should be able to finish the translation of the Nabak New Testament this year." A two-year schedule formed in my mind and I recited:

"Finish all the major checks this year.

Proofread and typeset next year.

Celebrate with the Nabak people before you two graduate from high school and return to the U.S.A. for college."

I looked around the table. The twins had seldom seen their mom this bubbly at breakfast. "It's do-able!" I exclaimed. "After 24 years on the project, at last, the end is in sight."

"Let's get on with it," Edmund said. "I'll easily finish chapter 12 this morning." And he headed to the office.

"Go for it, Mom," the twins said as they cleared the table and grabbed up their books for school.

But that was this morning. Edmund was alive and warm. Now, this afternoon, something dreadful, something unimaginable had ruptured my well-planned world.

His computer screen showed verses in I Corinthians 13, the love chapter. I gasped. *How ironic that love would be his focus in that one split second when someone plunged an axe into the back of his head.* I was not ready for murder. *This was incomprehensible. I was brought up in a loving, Christian home. I never wanted anything but to serve God and do good to others. I was a Bible translator, for crying out loud.*

My house was in order, the checkbook was balanced. I read my Bible every day...went to church. How could doing everything right turn out like this? Didn't murder happen to foolish people who were in wrong places, doing wrong things?

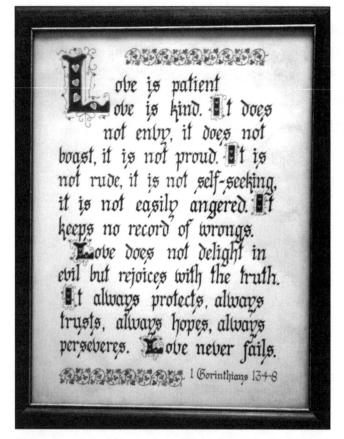

This copy of the famous love chapter hangs in the Fabian's living room.

Calligraphy by Wendy Richards

❈ CHAPTER THREE

A strange twist

"Be near when I am dying
O show thy Cross to me!
And, for my succor flying,
Come, Lord, to set me free.
These eyes, new faith receiving,
From Thee shall never move;
For he who dies believing
Dies safely in Thy love."[5]

Within minutes two doctors from our mission center clinic arrived at the house. They transported Edmund to the clinic and said they would call for me soon.

In the midst of the hubbub Kurt arrived home early from school. Someone had met him on the road and told him, "Your father has been in an accident." Kurt saw several vehicles in the yard and a commotion at the door of his dad's office. He walked in just in time to see the medical staff place his dad on a stretcher. As they carried him out he saw the rug soaked with blood.

I turned, surprised to see Kurt surveying the scene. "Someone attacked Daddy," I blurted out.

Our security officer took us to his home. Soon our mission's mem-

---

[5] Gerhardt, Paul. "O Sacred Head, Now Wounded."

ber care person arrived. But just then the phone rang and the two men said, "It's the clinic. You should go there now."

Kurt and I walked on a footpath across our mission center. "Daddy and I will have to go to Australia. It's a huge injury," I said. I didn't know what else to say.

"Maybe they can sew it up here. I hope they hurry," he said.

At the clinic, Dr. Helen led us into her office. I knew immediately that she bore bad news. She spoke tenderly. She held my hand while delivering her report, "I'm so sorry, Grace. Edmund is brain dead." She could not restrain the tears. "You can be sure he never felt a thing."

Then Dr. Doreen, a trauma center doctor visiting our mission center for a few weeks, added, "Even if you had been in the most up-to-date emergency facility back in America, it would not have helped. There is nothing we can do for him." *How could such kindhearted people say such ghastly words? Was there really no hope he could be saved?*

They walked us to the emergency room where Edmund lay, still breathing. They had removed his bloody shirt. If I hadn't known that his head was split open, I would have thought he was sleeping. But the stainless steel pail on the floor under the head of the stretcher, gave it away. Drops of blood splattered into it, like the first raindrops on our tin roof.

Heidi, Kurt's twin sister, heard the news at school and ran to join us. So much can happen in just a few seconds. How could I tell her this? I held her tight and told her very simply, "Someone attacked Daddy. He's dying," I said.

As Kurt and Heidi and I sat at the clinic beside Edmund, the blood dribbled into that pail.

We looked at his scar-covered body, all from past surgeries—an appendectomy, torn cartilage in his knees, jaw surgery, a bad cut on his thumb. A huge scar on his chest where his gall bladder had been removed looked rough and hurtful. We couldn't see the scar on his back where surgeons had put in a stainless steel plate, but we knew it was there.

Edmund was a male nurse, always eager to save others; now he couldn't save himself. Pain was not a new phenomenon for Edmund. Not a day passed without distress. And now this.

I could hear the steady *drip, drip, drip* of blood.

I felt no desire to squeeze his hand and say, "I love you." He wasn't there. This was just the shell.

He was brain dead, murdered. One moment he had wrestled with translating the word "love," the next moment he had knelt, saturated with the very presence of the God who said, "I am the perfect image of eternal love." *Edmund, I can't feel sorry for you. But I do feel sorry for me.*

We, by some strange twist of Divine Providence, had suddenly been thrust into circumstances we could never have imagined and certainly would not have chosen. Watching his body shut down was unspeakably horrible.

Just a few days earlier in one of those rare moments when Edmund talked about the aches in his body, I jokingly said to him, "Oh, honey, you'll probably live to be as old as my dad (91 years old at the time). And I, who have never had a pain in my whole life, will be the first to go."

"No, Grace," he responded. "It won't be like that." I shrugged it off at the time, but now as I sat in a daze in the clinic, his words flashed before me. *Did he have a sense of what would happen?*

Drip, drip, the drops of blood fell. Why did it sound louder now to my ears?

Everything that meant anything to me paraded before me in a millisecond, like a grainy home movie:

—A bell ringing in the steeple of the church across the road where I grew up in Otego, New York...

—My parents kneeling and praying with my sisters and me in the living room before we hopped on the school bus...

—Edmund escorting me down the aisle on our wedding day in 1967...

—Our arrival in the spectacular country of Papua New Guinea on July 4, 1969, not with a bang but with a quiet passion to reach the Nabak people...

Heidi sat in the waiting room with her classmates, praying. Her twin brother Kurt, who resembled his father, couldn't leave my side. I was comforted by their presence. We could read the love and pain in each other's eyes. As their mother, I had always tried to shield them from hurts, but I was powerless to prevent this. *Moms can't fix some things.*

And their dad, the self-appointed director of the family, couldn't fix it either. No directives, "No, you can't," "Finish up," "Hurry up," "Behave yourself," came from him now as he lay motionless on his back, eyes closed.

We phoned to break the news to our two children in America. How would our oldest son Jonathan respond to his father's death? I could only dimly imagine the shock he and his wife Amy would feel. Our daughter Dietlinde would graduate this very week from Houghton College. *Oh, God, help them, steady them. Show us the way.* Four vibrant, buoyant children. I knew this loss would irrevocably change our lives, setting us on a track down which we had to journey whether we were ready to or not. *What would the future hold?*

Drip, drip, drip.

Then followed the robotic phone calls to my dear father, my sisters, Edmund's family in Germany, and supporting churches.

One of the nurses offered us sodas. We took them but then looked at each other. "This isn't a party," Kurt whispered. We only drank sodas in the Fabian family to celebrate someone's birthday. This was no party. No, it was the shocking, unspeakable agony of watching the life of the one we loved torn from us—the man I had been married to for 25 years, eight months and three days.

As one hour stretched to two, pauses in Edmund's breathing became more frequent. Graciously, the doctor gave Edmund medication to prevent spasms or twitching in his body. But still the soft *drip, drip, drip* went on. Another hour. His breathing became more irregular. *How long does it take for a body to be drained of its blood?*

One more hour of ragged, increasingly shallow breathing. Sometimes it was like apnea. There would be a long pause of 45 seconds or more with no breath. "How long can this go on?" I asked Jill, one of the nurses.

She explained that the brain stem regulates heartbeat and breathing. "Since the brain stem was not severed, he continues to breathe. His heart continues to beat even though he's brain dead."

With the *drip, drip, drip,* the truth of Edmund's death slowly seeped into our brains. It is one thing for someone to deliver the death sentence; it is quite another thing to accept the reality.

Into this hazy state of bewilderment a surprising voice from deep inside of me surfaced. Just as Dr. Helen had held my hand in her office, I now felt a hand on my shoulder to compel my attention. It was one of those rare occasions when God whispered to me. Though not audible, the words were unmistakably His. He said, "Grace, the way you respond to all of this is very important." The unbidden words resonated powerfully and firmly deep within. My heart told me it was a revelation of sorts. Before my mind could question the words, a merciful calm enveloped me. I knew in an unexplainable way, that God's tender strength was all around us.

I turned my attention back to my children. Now it was six o'clock. We had reached the point where we merely waited for the end of this vigil. *"Just take him, Lord,"* I prayed. Finally, four hours after the catastrophe, his breathing ceased. Dr. Helen looked at the clock and wrote "7:15 P.M." on the death certificate. On the line, "Cause of death," she wrote, "head injury due to blow to the head by an axe." What we had known for four long hours was now official, documented on death certificate #74,363.

❊ CHAPTER FOUR
Who did it?

"There are occasional moments in life
when God gets my absolute attention.
Like when the engine quits on takeoff at 800
feet over a busy city.
Or the fuel tank runs dry.
Or ice forms on the wings faster than you can measure.
Or you run out of runway and experience at the same time."[6]

Back home the house smelled of stale coffee. When I had looked out my office window this afternoon there was sunlight. Now it was dark. I switched on a light and wished for a fire in the fireplace...anything to cheer me. The stench of death hung in the air.

Even speaking took too much effort. The twins and I knew how the other felt. It wasn't a time for words anyway. We wanted each other for sure, but we needed quiet. Words would be a violation somehow.

I headed to the bedroom. It looked the same as when I had left it in the morning, except now my bloody skirt lay crumpled and sickly in the corner. I had thrown it there before heading off to the clinic. The sight of it now pushed a replay button in my head, and before I knew it, the painful scene in the office flashed back to repel me. My stomach lurched. I rushed to the bathroom and retched in the toilet.

---

[6] May, Bernie. *Under His Wing*. Orlando: Wycliffe, 1986: 36.

Before today that skirt had been my favorite. Not now. I dunked the stained garment in the sink to soak in cold water. As I staggered back to the bedroom I wondered why I hadn't simply thrown it in the garbage. I knew I would never wear that outfit again.

My sewing machine with an assortment of sewing notions stood on my desk under the front windows of the bedroom, but my eyes turned instinctively to the other side of the room, to Edmund's worktable. I picked up a knick-knack from the center of his desk, a little decorative mirror one of the children had given him for Christmas. At the time, all of us marveled that an artist could paint a miniature scene on a 3x4 inch mirror. It showed a lighthouse standing on a rocky shore. A tree stood to the left of the lighthouse, its branches leafless, bent over in the wind. The designer had carefully etched these words in the sky above the thrashing waves: "Thou Wilt Keep Him in Perfect Peace, Whose Mind is Stayed on Thee. Isaiah 26:3." *Your attention is riveted on that Prince of Peace right now, isn't it, Edmund?* In this murky atmosphere of chaos and horror I could only dimly imagine what it would be like to be bathed with perfect peace.

A tiny pile of birthday cards on the corner of the table beckoned me. Edmund's 57th birthday was just five days away. These few greetings from friends and family had already arrived. Kurt and Heidi had said he mustn't open them until his birthday. I opened the white envelope from Dawn, our dear friend and prayer warrior. "I make all things new,"[7] the card read. I read it again. *For you, dear Edmund, this promise has been literally fulfilled today.*

Then I glanced at the little pile of books off to the side. Edmund used these resources when teaching German, his mother tongue, at the high school for missionaries' kids. I was almost afraid to touch it. It seemed sacred now. The cover of one note-

[7] Revelation 21:5

book carried his life verse, "Teach us to number our days that we may apply our hearts to wisdom."[8]

A knock at the door broke my reverie. Lee, my friend, came and sat quietly beside me in our living room. She put her arm around me. Heidi's schoolmate and best friend Mindy also came to spend the night.

Kurt took on the responsibilities of his father. We affectionately called Edmund "The Checker" because he always examined the house at night: doors locked, security alarm on, cat out, lights off—a little ritual he performed each night. Kurt dutifully locked the doors then plucked up courage to go down to the office and make sure that that door was locked.

I couldn't stomach the thought of entering Edmund's office tonight. Someday I would have to clean up the terrible mess, but I couldn't face it just yet. Kurt finished his father's rounds and returned to the bedroom. "Someone cleaned up the mess," he said. We found out later that our friends, the McGuckins, had performed this task for us, certainly a labor of love on our behalf.

"Thank you, Kurt, for checking." We lay down on top of my bed holding hands, drawing strength from each other.

Then Kurt voiced the question that probably everyone on the mission center was asking. "Who did it, Mom?" We both felt afraid to face that question. We were confused and tired. We stared at the ceiling in disbelief.

"I don't know, Kurt. I don't know." My heart ached. "All I do know at this point is that God is utterly dependable...but that's all I know. I won't ever doubt that."

"But how did it happen?"

"I don't know."

"Did you see anything?"

"Only this. I was sitting at my desk with Kayak beside me. I was busy entering corrections to the manuscript of Titus. I told

8 Psalm 90:12

Kayak that we'd stop for coffee break as soon as I finished this last verse. Kayak excused himself to go to the bathroom. As he walked down through the office where Daddy and Miliŋnâŋe worked, he jokingly said to them, 'You two working hard? The coffee's perking. You can't have any if you aren't working!' "

"You overheard him say that? So obviously there was nothing out of the ordinary at that point. Then what happened?"

"Well, Kayak went on his way and I finished typing that verse. As I stood to go to the kitchen and pour the coffee, Miliŋnâŋe ran past the window."

"Isn't that odd? I don't remember ever seeing a Nabak man running, except on the soccer field."

"I called out *Geŋ zigok? What's up?*" He didn't answer. He just kept running toward the road. I guessed that he and Daddy had seen vandals breaking in the neighbor's house."

"It wouldn't be the first time we've seen foul play next door, especially since the Stuckys are out in their village and the house is unoccupied."

"'Probably he's going to head off the vandals from the front', is what I thought at the time. Then I asked Daddy if there was a problem again next door."

"And there was no answer, right?"

"No answer. I rolled back my office chair and looked over to the office. The door between our two rooms stood open. I expected to see the office empty, thinking Daddy must have gone across the yard in the back to catch those vandals red-handed. But instead..."

"I know, Mom, you don't have to say it."

"Kurt, I don't know how the axe got there. Who would have done such an awful thing?"

The question hung in the air unanswered.

Chapter Five

The unfaceable

"How do we come to face the unfaceable, talk about the unspeakable?"[9]

In the morning, the large mission center, located on a piece of land leased to us by the government of Papua New Guinea as a place to do linguistic research, came alive. Hundreds of missionaries lived here. The printing presses spit out Scripture portions in a multitude of languages, Land Rovers received make-overs at the mechanics shop, and Cessnas and helicopters took off for distant airstrips where missionary translators and literacy workers waited for mail and supplies. This was the hub for hundreds of translators spread from the coral atolls to the Indonesian border. Hundreds of missionaries' kids attended school here.

Edmund and I owned a house here, but rented it out to other missionaries while we lived with the Nabak people. Periodically we returned to the Center for workshops, opportunities to meet with other co-workers who helped us unravel the mysteries of the complicated Nabak grammar. Sometimes we devised primers for teaching the Nabaks to read or we might be attending anthropology seminars designed to help us reach across cultural barriers.

But this morning attending a workshop or zipping ahead on translation was the farthest thought from our minds. A dark cloud

[9] Miller, Sue. *The Story of My Father.* New York: Random House, 2003: 183.

overshadowed the usually energetic base of operations. The shocking news of Edmund's death spread from house to house, and from the communication center to two-way radios out in distant villages.

As a community of mostly expatriates, and all believers in Christ, we experienced a definite camaraderie, even though we came from seventeen different countries. My children called several of the adults "aunt" and "uncle." The other missionaries' children were as close to them as sisters and brothers. When one member of our community hurt, everyone felt it.

Danger, threats and hardship in this foreign land were not a surprising occurrence to us. But to be murdered at the translation desk? That was, well, outrageous!

These dear brothers and sisters in Christ now encircled us with love and concern. They visited, bringing food, wishing they could somehow ease our pain. They listened patiently as I told them my suspicions of thugs from a nearby village coming to the office door and throwing an axe at Edmund.

When someone mentioned that Miliŋnâŋe was in jail, I assumed that the police had put him there for protection. I believed Miliŋnâŋe had witnessed the crime.

One of the visitors asked about Zumbek. "Yes, we notified him last night. He said he'd come down as soon as possible." Zumbek, a young Nabak man, had lived with us, and had become a Christ follower during an evangelistic outreach. He expressed a desire to go to Bible College and we encouraged him and supported him financially.

Then he continued his education at seminary. He married a beautiful Christian lady, Egue, and together they went to Germany to represent the Lutheran Church. He now lived in a different part of Papua New Guinea, where he taught at a

Lutheran Seminary. We notified Zumbek, and almost immediately he jumped on public transport. He traveled half the night and half the next day. He arrived bedraggled, bewildered and in a state of shock.

As Zumbek ate the hearty lunch I had prepared, and downed several cups of coffee, we told him the strange details of Edmund's death. After more hugs and sobbing he announced, "I need to go and talk with Miliŋnâŋe."

Evening approached but he was determined to find another truck going to Kainantu, the nearby town where Miliŋnâŋe had been placed in a holding cell.

When Zumbek returned from the jail that evening, he told me, "Miliŋnâŋe said to come back tomorrow and he'll tell me everything. He doesn't want to talk about it in the dark."

Saturday dawned, another day of speculation, of questions. Someone suggested that Miliŋnâŋe was the criminal. "You're wrong," I said. "He's one of our co-translators. He was headmaster of the primary school in the village. Why! Every Friday he sat around this very table and played dominoes with us." Then, as an afterthought, I said, "Besides, the Nabak people don't fight and kill."

Our regional director, who had visited the Nabak people, agreed with me that it was very unlikely that a crime of such magnitude would be committed by a Nabak.

Kayak, however, was very distraught. As we stood outside talking about the events of that fateful Thursday, he said, "Miliŋnâŋe is a traitor; he's a Judas!"

"You didn't see it, so you can't really say," I countered. I stood up for Miliŋnâŋe, our friend and co-translator, thoroughly convinced that he could not possibly be the one behind this heinous crime.

When Zumbek returned from his second visit to the jail, he was strangely quiet and asked me, "Did you see any strangers in the backyard on Thursday afternoon?"

"No, but in the morning there were two young men attempting to break in next door at Stucky's house."

"Did Edmund mention anything to you about problems as he worked with Miliŋnâŋe?" *What was Zumbek fishing for anyway?*

"Uuhhh, actually he did tell me that sometimes Miliŋnâŋe is a brilliant co-translator, but that at other times, he seems distracted. Edmund said that he didn't know what the problem was, but that he wouldn't invite Miliŋnâŋe to come back after his six week's break. He would find someone else to come in his place to rotate with the other Nabak co-translators."

Zumbek turned, without a word, and left the house.

That afternoon the director of our Papua New Guinea branch called me to his office. Zumbek was already there. So was our regional assistant director. *Am I here to talk about funeral arrangements? All these men are my friends. Why do I suddenly feel a premonition, a sense of danger?*

The branch director opened the conversation. "We asked Zumbek to tell us about his visit yesterday at the jail. And now we've asked you to come so you can hear the report also," he said. *Strange, why wouldn't Zumbek tell me directly?*

In true Nabak conversational style, Zumbek did not come immediately to the point. First, he talked about the importance of our translation work. He expressed his shock at hearing the news of Edmund's death. Finally, he maneuvered the conversation to the jail visit. He was obviously trying to find a way to tell me something. Then with carefully chosen words, as gently as was possible, Zumbek said, "Miliŋnâŋe confessed to killing Edmund."

My breath went out of me. The pain of these brutal facts pierced my heart like an arrow, and lodged there. Chills ricocheted up and down my spine. My whole body trembled. The men quickly braced me, as I was reeling, losing my balance.

How could it be that Edmund was slaughtered by one of the very people we had learned to love, the people for whom we were translating the Bible? Zumbek gathered me in his arms, his sobs joining mine.

With the pulse of the sobs, questions throbbed in my heart like the beating of a Nabak drum. *Why did he do it? Why? Why? Why? What will the children think when they hear this news? Will they hate Papua New Guineans? Will they be bitter? Or worse yet, will they lose their faith?* I turned toward home to tell them.

How? How? How did we come to be here anyway?

How could it be that Edmund was kept safe through the horrors of World War II, only to be hacked down in our own home?

Edmund and Miliŋnâŋe together in 1986.

❦ CHAPTER SIX

Chosen to live

"If in the paths of the world
Stones might have wounded thy feet,
Toil and dejection have tried
Thy spirit, of that we saw nothing.
To us thou wast still
Cheerful and helpful and firm....
Languor is not in your heart,
Weakness is not in your word,
Weariness not on your brow."[10]

Edmund, the man whose analytical style made him an ideal candidate for linguistics and translation, believed that God had called him, and I knew he was "turned on." For sure he came to this field of study by a circuitous route, but definitely by the hand of God.

People sent sympathy cards when they heard the news of Edmund's death. Our co-workers out in the villages sent messages to us over the two-way radio. A stack of e-mails and faxes came from others who had heard the news of Edmund's death.

Many of the letters mentioned their memories of Edmund and of how he had blessed them in some way. We cried as we read the words, "We are weeping with you."

[10] Arnold, Matthew, Rugby Chapel. quoted in Elliot, Elisabeth. *A Chance to Die*. New Jersey: Fleming H. Revell, 1987: 225.

Some wrote that they remembered his testimony from when we visited their churches, and how they were touched by it. One friend wrote, "I wish I could remember everything Edmund said about his family fleeing from the Russians."

We were grateful that the Lord had put it on our minds a few years earlier to record Edmund sharing his story. It happened one evening as we sat in the home of Dick and Thelma Williams in Binghamton, New York. Dick and Thelma had invited a few people from their church to join us for refreshments after the evening service. We gathered in the den downstairs. A fire blazed in the fireplace. Thelma, the queen of all hostesses, passed around a plate of vegetables and dip. Then an assortment of nuts, pretzels and brownies. Dick was the coffee man. Everyone chatted happily. Edmund and I were glad for this opportunity to meet people in this relaxed atmosphere.

We had just finished showing slides at Calvary Baptist Tabernacle, one of our supporting churches. People listened attentively to my story of a new believer, Zumbek, among the Nabak people. Edmund closed the meeting with a brief testimony of growing up in Poland, fleeing during the war and how God had led us to Papua New Guinea.

Now, as we relaxed in Dick and Thelma's home, one of the guests mentioned that he had fought in France in World War II. "How did your family manage to get out of Poland?" he asked.

"Oh, I thought you were German," Doris said.

By now everyone was seated with coffee cups and plates of snacks. Dick reached around to the counter and clicked on the tape recorder.

Edmund began. "My German passport says that I was born in Janufka, in the province of Rowno, Poland. I remember asking my parents at the supper table one evening, 'How come we're Germans but we live in Poland?'"

"Papa gave me a little history lesson. He said that Catherine the Great in 1763 invited people from Europe to come to Russia in the hopes of introducing farming skills and culture to the people. Thousands of Germans, including our ancestors, migrated here to homestead." Papa went on to tell us how the very area where we lived had been divided and occupied by many nations throughout history, and that the borders of Russia and Poland had changed several times.

As a child, I couldn't follow it all, but I knew that by the time I was born, in 1936, that area belonged to Poland. Even with these territorial changes we German immigrants always kept our identity as German citizens.

"Oh, so that's how, even though you were born in Poland, you're still German,' Doris said.

Edmund nodded. He obviously felt comfortable with everyone's attention so he continued. "My father, Albert Fabian, was a grocer. Both he and my mother, Amalie nee Hennig, worked extremely hard and long hours to make a success of the business there in Poland.

"I was the fourth of six children. We all grew up bilingual, speaking Polish and German. Each of us children, in time, learned different parts of the retail business and worked alongside our parents.

"Then the war! All of a sudden in 1939 Germany invaded Poland. Hitler and Stalin decided to divide Poland in half. The part where we lived, near the Russian border, would be absorbed into the Soviet Union. The western half the Germans incorporated into the Reich. All of us Germans were evacuated to central Poland. This move interrupted our schooling, and setting up a grocery business again proved difficult with severe shortages everywhere.

"Shortages and rules. The government required that we post a sign 'Forbidden to Jews' outside our shop. As a child I didn't understand what that was all about. I only knew that certain children in my neighborhood, children I played with, mysteriously disappeared or now attended a different school.

"News spread through rumors, since the police confiscated our radios. Worrying letters arrived from our relatives back in Germany. To our horror, my father received a draft notice. It was compulsory that he enlist in the military and serve in the German army. He was shipped out immediately to France, leaving behind six frightened children who needed a father. Mama wondered how she could balance business and her family."

Yvonne, one of the guests, mentioned that her mother and father came from Germany. "What you're saying, Edmund, reminds me of some of my parents' stories. It was horrific all right." She motioned for Edmund to continue.

Edmund looked down as a tsunami of emotions flooded over him. "Yes," he said quietly. "I don't have enough adjectives to describe the war years. But every time those scenes come back to haunt me, there is one image that rises to the top. It is the picture of my Mama on her knees in prayer.

She prayed aloud and with tears—prayers that still echo in my heart. 'Bring Papa home soon,' she'd say. 'Give us our daily bread. Send your guardian angels. Give me strength...' I hated to see Mama cry, but when she stood after her prayer vigils, her face was bright and serene. That image burned itself into my soul. Naturally, I turned to her whenever I was frightened, which was often.

"Everyone else in my world, it seemed to me, was either deep in thought or sad. Where had the carefree days of school, playing ball and laughing gone? We all worked hard—weeding, canning, mending, cooking. There was never any time to slow down if we wanted to survive. My mother's calloused, overworked hands, and the loss of my father are two of my strong childhood memories."

Harold, one of the guests sitting across from Edmund, motioned for Edmund to stop. "I'm deeply moved by your story." He looked around the circle, "And we thought it was tough in this country to have gas and sugar rationed." Then looking at Edmund he said, "But you, you were right in the thick of it."

I was almost hoping to change the subject or bring the evening to a conclusion to spare Edmund more pain but I could feel the vibes of love coming from everyone in the room. Evidently, he could sense the support too because he took a deep breath and continued.

"I found the cold, wet winters the hardest. It was dismal because blackout paper replaced my mother's pretty lace curtains and potted plants at the windows. Karl and Else, my oldest brother and sister, brought home stories of steel-plated army trucks roaring through the streets, loaded with arrested people. The only news we heard was bad; never a letup.

"But stronger than the images of raids and atrocities was this bright image of Mama worshipping. She sat bent over reading her Bible by the flickering light of an oil lamp. She read aloud, haltingly, then prayed and sang. Often I saw tears in her eyes. Always at the end, a look of calm and hope. Could such a simple thing as prayer really make any difference when such staggering events are happening in your own backyard, I wondered?"

Edmund had difficulty continuing. In telling the story he relived the horrifying tales of his childhood. I took his hand. "She was an amazing woman," I said.

Thelma brought him a glass of water. "Thank you," he said. But there was a lump in his throat. He took a drink and continued. "But it gets worse. In 1944 the Russian soldiers advanced closer and closer to our city. As if it were not enough to worry about what was happening in France, now we were no longer on the periphery of this world war; shots were being fired in the street outside our door.

On rare occasions my parents reminisced about their experiences in World War I, when they were taken deep into Russian Siberia, to the labor camps. Judging from those stories of hardship, we all realized how horrendous it would be if we were captured by the Russian soldiers.

"One day as Mama knelt praying, we heard the low rumble of artillery. I looked to Mama for an explanation. Ashen-faced, she jumped up and cried, 'It's the Russians.' I held both hands over my ears. Explosions, air-raid sirens, terror!

I rushed to Mama. My little sister screamed. Else asked, "What shall we do, Mama?" We were absolutely vulnerable, with no transportation, no man in the house, no weapons. Every train station near us had been bombed. We were trapped. Mama had sensed the danger because she pulled out the cedar chest and we could see it was half full. She immediately put us to work gathering other items to pack. She fitted in all of our valuable possessions, including my parents' wedding presents. She calmed us, "God will protect us." We watched as she slipped a few coins into a little silk pouch she had made. It had two buttonholes and she carefully fastened it inside her blouse."

"By the way," I said, "we still have that little silk pouch and the coins. It's a legacy she left Edmund."

Edmund smiled. "When I hold it I think of how she worked and prepared for the inevitable.

One day my older brother rushed in. 'The Russian soldiers are advancing from the east. People say they're scarcely five kilometers away!' How could we possibly get out alive?

"As thin and fragile as Mama was, she clung fiercely to her faith. 'Our only recourse is praying to a God who can't let us down,' she said. She totally staked her life and the lives of us children on this hope.

"God's answer came in the form of a troop of starving, bedraggled German soldiers. They fled just ahead of the Russian soldiers. It seems that Hitler's idea of a *blitzkrieg* had backfired. Now the German soldiers were on the run.

When they saw the German sign for our grocery store, they stopped and begged for food. 'You can have any of the food from our store you want, But!' she said, blocking the doorway, 'in exchange take us to the next open train station!' She put her shoulders back to stand her full five feet, and raised her arms blocking the doorway. Hearing the rumble of Russian artillery growing louder in the background, the desperate soldiers agreed to her terms.

"Slipping and sliding in the snow they carried out every jar of fruit and vegetables we had bottled that summer. Two of the soldiers lugged the crock of sauerkraut out to the truck. Others grabbed the homemade sausages and threw them into the truck. They literally cleared out everything from our store. In the backyard we were fattening two pigs. The soldiers hoisted them onto the truck too.

"Else, my oldest sister, now 15, the one who could wait on the customers so efficiently, grabbed up my five-year-old sister, Getrud, and hopped onto the back of the truck. Karl, my 13-year-old brother, who often worked with my father loading the wagon with vegetables from the farmer's market, now boosted Ferdinand, age seven, onto the army truck. I was nine and managed to scramble up. I looked around for Lilly. At only 11 years of age, she could count money and make the right change for customers. She soon joined us with a sly smirk on her face. 'I emptied the cash register when the soldiers weren't looking,' she whispered. Then she lifted her apron pocket to show us her stash.'"

There was a lot of laughter in the den as Edmund described the little scene in the store in Poland with Lilly and her money. I don't think any of us realized until then how somber the atmosphere had become. I was aware that I'd been sitting on the edge of my chair riveted on Edmund's story, and I was glad for the break in tension. Dick put on another pot of coffee.

"Did I tell you that it was a harsh winter?"

We shook our heads as we shifted positions.

"I remember distinctly that the snow pelted us," he said. "But, as usual, Mama orchestrated the whole evacuation process. Last of all, following her instructions, the soldiers carried out Mama's precious cedar chest and shoved it next to the heap of groceries that had once been our flourishing business. Ignoring the shouts of the soldiers, '*Schnell! Schnell!*' she took a quick head count. Only when absolutely positive that all six of us were accounted for did Mama climb in.

"Immediately we huddled under the two feather blankets Mama had grabbed at the last minute, grateful for the warmth they provided. Mama sighed with relief as we moved out of the danger zone. How could she know that this was the beginning of months of running for our lives?

⚔ CHAPTER SEVEN

The crazy woman

"In Christ alone my hope is found.
He is my light, my strength, my song;
This Cornerstone, this solid ground,
Firm through the fiercest drought and storm.
What heights of love; what depths of peace,
When fears are stilled, when strivings cease.
My comforter, my all in all,
Here in the love of Christ I stand." [11]

"After a stomach-lurching trip in the back of that army truck, for what seemed to be an eternity, we arrived at a little country railroad terminal. Hundreds of people, if not thousands, milled about on the platform. In the midst of this chaos we heard the words, 'Only one more train, only one more train,' repeated over and over. One more finally did arrive, but there was such a stampede of people clambering onto it that our little family could not make it.

"As the train pulled out I saw the look on my mother's face: anguish. Would there ever be a train for us? Mama knelt on the steps of the train station and prayed aloud. Onlookers shrugged and turned away from this 'poor, crazy woman.' Others looked on in sheer amazement. Wasn't it utter rubbish to believe that God was listening? Didn't she know about the heartbreaks, the horrific

---

[11] Getty, Keith and Stuart Townend. "In Christ Alone." Thankyou Music. 2002.

events, the annihilation of children, family and friends? 'Poor disillusioned soul,' they murmured. In my little heart I knew she was not crazy. She was my Mama and I loved her."

Several of us wiped tears from our eyes as we listened to Edmund speak of his mother. Some of us were mothers and felt the emotion of this scene. We could only dimly imagine what this little family suffered.

With a husky voice Edmund continued, "All night we shivered outside in the freezing cold, hoping against hope for another train to come. The hours dragged by. Our feet grew numb and our stomachs growled. There was no such thing as a train schedule. Chaos reigned.

"At the first sign of day in the east Mama roused us. We were groggy from sleep deprivation and hadn't heard the train. Surprisingly another train did come and my mother herded us toward one of the coal cars. How we managed to remain together with all the jostling and bedlam is a mystery. Perhaps it had something to do with those 'guardian angels' Mama constantly talked about. Somehow, we crammed into one corner of an open coal car.

"As the train puffed and hissed and pulled away, Mama looked back at her treasured trunk still on the train station steps. 'At least I have all of you,' I heard her say above the din and shoving. Then the train picked up speed. How the icy wind blew around us! We hid under the feather blankets, our only protection from the swirling coal dust and snow. The only thing that kept us from starvation was the food that Mama had frantically stuffed into a pillowcase.

"Many people had no covering and no food. The living threw the dead, the frozen, the starved bodies over the side of the coal car. Sometimes the train stopped so that the tracks could be cleared of dead bodies before it could proceed. We traveled only at night so we would not be spotted and bombed by the planes circling overhead. I was nine years old and the horrors I witnessed on that long trip are indelibly etched upon my mind and heart."

Edmund paused. I could tell that the images swirling through his brain brought excruciating memories. I had heard Edmund share parts of this story before, but I knew I would never really comprehend the severe trauma he had experienced. I grew sad realizing that the man I loved had endured so much. I understood for the first time why he always turned off the television when there was any movie about war. I knew why he sometimes woke up in the night because of nightmares. At the same time I felt proud of him that he had still succeeded in many areas of his life. I hoped and prayed that what had happened to him would never happen to our children.

"Finally, we reached Schlieren in western Poland," Edmund took up the story again. "We lived in a barn there for several months and helped a farmer in exchange for food. 'Head west' became our watchword, the goal of all of us miserable refugees. But trekking west proved almost impossible. Most trains and tracks were destroyed, so to continue our journey we traveled in a caravan of horse-drawn wagons. No grain for feed meant that the horses were weak and unable to pull heavy loads. Only the elderly, pregnant women, and little children were allowed to ride on the wagons. My brothers and sisters and I joined the other young people and the men, tramping ahead of the wagons. We helped clear the road of dead people and dead animals—the result of the previous day's bombing. So many rotting corpses were strewn everywhere. The stench was terrible.

"Eventually, we reached the American Zone. By this time, we were so exhausted and disheveled we could barely stand in the long line at the Red Cross refugee office. We finally filled out the information—our names and former address.

But our relief at finding shelter and hot food was short-lived because just at that time the United States agreed to give this city over to Russia in exchange for part of Berlin. So once again we stood in territory occupied by the Russian troops and governed by Communists.

And once again, Mama prayed, 'Almighty God, hear our prayers, save us. Give me grace for what lies ahead.'

As she prayed we could hear Russian soldiers pounding on doors at night demanding girls. She kept praying aloud as we listened to the cries and screams from the other houses up and down the street. We learned that these lustful, drunken soldiers broke in and searched under beds and in closets. Always, there knelt Mama praying aloud to her God.

Mama spoke Russian and served as an interpreter for the Russian officers. When these ruthless soldiers approached our shelter, my three sisters hid. My mother, never a weakling, bravely strode to the door. Without a tremor, she spoke to the soldiers in Russian saying that she was going to report them to the official for whom she worked. The soldiers left, and in this way my sisters were kept from being raped."

"What a brave, ingenious woman she was," said Donna. We all agreed.

"I don't know how long we walked, hiding and struggling through woods and streams," Edmund said, almost as if he were asking a question. "In my memory it was just endless tramping. We could finally see Berlin in the distance. But it was not Berlin as we imagined it. Instead, what we saw was a wall of fire. Nothing but holocaust! We could go no farther.

"Recently I read a quotation from Truman's diary about his visit to Germany. I think his words were 'a long, never-ending procession of men, women and children, all staring straight ahead, carrying what they could of their belongings to nowhere in particular."[12] He couldn't have said it better.

"In Berlin we heard the announcement of Admiral Doenitz that Germany had surrendered to the Allies. Had our soldier Papa survived? Was he in a prison camp? Or was he like one of those corpses we had seen on our flight? Little did we know that he was heading north trying to find us."

"Through the International Red Cross, Papa learned of our whereabouts. Imagine our delight when Papa showed up one day! Tears flowed freely. He said that Berlin was going to be divided. Just days before the border patrol was set up, Papa secretly led us, under cover of darkness, across *Niemandsland* (no-man's-land) to what became known as West Berlin.

"There were many hard years after the war as we regrouped as a family and started over again from scratch to build our family's grocery business. We had nothing but the rags on our bodies and little knapsacks on our backs. Our education was in shambles, but our whole family had been spared many of the atrocities others had experienced.

"Now I look back and marvel at God's love and protection of our family. Through it all, Mama's prayers embraced us. I did not learn until years later that one quarter of the population of Poland died during World War II. Death narrowly missed us. Why were my sisters some of the few not molested? Why had I been spared?"

There was a reflective silence in the room. Nobody moved. "Your Mama's prayers were heard," Pat said, fully convinced of what he said.

"And she was no crazy woman," Pat's wife added.

"No, she wasn't," I said. "It was the world that had gone insane."

---

[12] Beschloss, Michael. *The Conquerors*. New York: Simon & Schuster, 2002: 255.

Dick turned off the tape recorder.

I couldn't help but think back to my tame childhood and what I was doing at nine years of age. How different Edmund's life was from my growing-up years.

In 1995 the Fabians visited Edmund's family in Germany on the way back to the US after Heidi and Kurt's graduation from High School in Papua New Guinea.

Upper Left to Right: Josef & Gertrud (E's sister) Nickels, Heidi, Grace, Amalie Fabian (Edmund's mother), Rudi & Lilli (E's sister) Schendel, Kurt
Lower Left to Right: Martina and daughter, Amy holding Isaac, Jonathan

☒ Chapter Eight

Building Blocks

"Every person we have ever known,
every place we have ever seen,
everything that has ever happened to us—
it all lives and breathes deep within us somewhere..."[13]

I lay flat on the cold linoleum floor of my bedroom leaning as close as possible to the stovepipe. Through the little holes in the base of the pipe I could make out most of the conversation downstairs. Daddy had fitted the tin pipe together and it curved up through the living room ceiling and on into the bedroom I shared with my sisters. Would my parents guess, even though I was upstairs and out of sight, that I eavesdropped on the conversation with our guest downstairs?

The black stove stood like the undisputed king of our living room. Every morning I could hear my father scraping the ashes through the grate, then shoveling the coal into its belly. As he rattled the vents and threw in a newspaper soaked with kerosene, I could almost predict the moment he tossed in the match. A day at the Jones household always started with that stove.

From our cozy spot under the quilts my sisters and I could hear the fire racing up through the stovepipe, roaring like some wild monster. That first KERBOOM was our signal to jump from the

---

[13] Buechner, Frederick. *A Room Called Remember.* New York: Harper & Row, 1984: 4.

beds, grab our clothes and charge down the stairs. Since the stove provided the only heat in the house we huddled around it to dress for school or church.

In the evening after dishes, piano practice, and homework were completed we again gathered around the plump stove with its cheerful fire. We held our flannel pajamas toward the stove to absorb its heat before hopping in them, and dashing upstairs to bed.

Inevitably the living room was where we entertained guests. Tonight we'd have to dress in our cold bedroom because my parents had invited a missionary to stay with us. "It's your bedtime, girls," my father had said, so I rather reluctantly had obeyed. *What was this mysterious yearning that kept me glued to hear Miss Byron's words?*

Oh, not just hers, but to any missionaries' words. Though I was too shy to say much at the dinner table when missionaries came to our home, you better believe I didn't miss a word. Secretly, I marveled at their ability to pronounce the names of strange places like Zimbabwe, Peddapalli and Nha Trang. Tribal groups like Witoto, Quechua, Shipibo or Dyak rolled off their tongues as easily as I could say Otego, New York, where we lived.

My father was the pastor of a little country church on Rural Delivery #2, better known to the locals as "the West Branch of the Otsdawa." I was eight years old when we moved to this farming community and I loved it. In Otego I began to feel carefree and protected.

But right now, stretched out on the bedroom floor, I felt cold. Not much warmth radiated from that stovepipe. I stretched to get the kinks out of my back, and crawled into bed. My feet quickly found the hot water bottle under the quilts. It was still warm and took the chill out of my toes. Just another reason for this secure and light feeling I had ever since moving here. I remembered that it had not always been this way.

I closed my eyes but instead of sleep I remembered back a few years before. When only five and a half, I, who always ran to Daddy to have my tears wiped away, now found my father in front of the bathroom mirror crying. I wrapped my little arms around his leg. "Daddy, why are you crying? What's the matter?"

My father, gentle person that he was, put down his shaver, rinsed off the shaving cream, then bent down and put his arms around me. "Gracie, Mommie has gone to heaven." His voice wavered and his eyes brimmed with tears.

I tried to get my mind around those words. Mommie had not been a big part of my life. My most vivid memory of her was as she stood behind an upstairs bay window, reaching her arms toward me and throwing kisses to me. I reached out for her embrace but I could only imagine it, for we were not allowed personal contact. Mommie had been moved to the Oswego County Tuberculosis Sanatorium in Richland, New York. The diagnosis of that "dread disease" came just a year after my little sister, Mary Christine, was born. I was four.

My three older sisters, Arloween, Kathryn, and Carmilla became my surrogate mothers, though they too struggled with the fact that Mommie could not be present in our home. Mommie died at age 40 on August 27, 1943 just months before streptomycin, an effective treatment for the disease, was discovered.

I turned over and pulled the quilts under my chin. Another family picture bubbled up into my memory. Sorrow was not an unknown phenomenon to our family, and then another thought followed. Neither was forgiveness unknown. I knew every detail of the story. In 1936 my sister, Martha Mai, was struck by a state trooper going 70 miles an hour in a school zone. No siren warned her of his approach. My pastor-father stood in our yard and saw it happen. He picked up her crushed three-year-old body and gently carried her inside.

This happened before I was born, but it was part of our family's history. I felt like I knew Martha Mai from the stories told, and from seeing her beautiful face in a large photograph hanging in a prominent place in our home. At the time, my father was pastor at the Kingsbury Baptist Church in upstate New York. In the courtroom he spoke words of forgiveness to the man who killed Martha Mai.

A few tears rolled down the side of my face and onto the pillow. It seemed like some little record in my head was turning and turning. Another flashback. I remembered that after my mother's death Daddy became both father and mother to us five girls. This took every bit of energy, ingenuity, and wisdom he could muster. We moved to a small farm in Coventryville, New York, where I loved to follow my father around the barn and fields. In my little mind I appointed myself as his caretaker. I reasoned that my mother had mysteriously disappeared, and if I didn't keep an eye out, maybe he would disappear also. So whether gathering sap to make maple syrup or feeding the calves, I trotted right behind him, helping as only a seven-year old can.

Those were the war years. My Aunt Ethel and my Grandma Jones came and helped out at the house so Daddy could work. My grandparents took baby Mary to their home, and my Aunt Lillie took care of Carmilla. We struggled with the fragmentation of our family, especially the loss of Mommie.

I was wide awake now. Like it happened yesterday I recalled the weekend my Aunt Lillie came to the farm and drove me to her house. All the way to Otego I chattered away telling her every Bible story I knew and singing every song Miss Tyler had taught us. I recited the memory verses like a pro. My aunt was impressed and asked Daddy how I had become so deeply grounded in God's Word.

"Miss Tyler," he said.

Miss Ruth Tyler was my Sunday School teacher. This retired school teacher dramatized the Bible stories and taught us songs, making the Bible come alive. Often she invited us to her home for games and our birthday parties. How I loved her. I smiled just thinking about her.

Like my father, Miss Tyler gave me a solid foundation on which to build a life of character and service for God. What a gift! God knew I needed a mother figure to fill the void in our family. *Thank you, Lord, for this demonstration of your unfailing love and care.*

Just last year, my father married my Aunt Lillie, his first wife's sister. I like to think that I had something to do with it, but probably not. I enjoyed seeing the look on people's faces when I told them, "I was the flower girl at my parents' wedding." And then I add, "My aunt became my step-mother and my cousin became my step-brother."

"I guess that makes your father your uncle," someone joked.

Oscar Burtch, Aunt Lillie's first husband, was pastor at First Christian Church in Otego, New York, when he died at age 27. The church, in a unique move, invited her to be their pastor. She agreed and successfully led that church for the next eighteen years. Now, with her marriage to my father, the church conveniently invited my father to be their new pastor.

Our new life as a blended family was not always easy, but I flourished in this more stable environment. Now our lives revolved around the church: ringing the bell, helping vacuum and dust the church, attending church suppers with the wonderful spread of baked beans, johnny cake, clam or chicken pies. Inevitably, a bountiful array of desserts would follow. My step-mother, whom

I now easily called "Mother", was the one who organized the games and programs, making the little white church with the red doors the center of our community.

The hot water bottle was no longer warm and I shoved it to the end of the bed. I knew I should be asleep by now but the thoughts came uninvited. One of the reasons I felt so light and free of worry since we moved to Otego was because of an important spiritual decision.

I recalled that night at Youth for Christ. The evangelist, Jack Wyrtzen, preached on the text, "For me to live is Christ and to die is gain."[14] He named sports, money, and popularity as causes people lived for. None of those passions applied to me at the young age of nine. Just the same, I knew in my heart of hearts that for me to live was not Christ. I sat between my parents as I confessed my sin. We prayed together. The counselor gave me a Gospel of John that I read straight through the next day. I filled in the card at the back—the date of my conversion, and a request for a New Testament. I hungrily read that too and sent in the card to receive a Bible. On that day in 1947, I started a journey full of adventure, one with the ever-present companionship of the Good Shepherd, and one I have never regretted.

Still sleep didn't come. I needed to reflect on the day's events. That Sunday morning in church Miss Byron, the visiting missionary, described a visit to a potter who lived near her bungalow in India. She said that he bought the clay, then trampled it in a pit with his bare feet to make it soft.

She explained how the potter had an exact idea of what he planned to make with the clay when he put it on the wheel. As he shaped it he would pick out the bits of grit or stone, and put it back in the pit and trample it some more, if necessary. Finally, when his molding was perfect, he placed it in the kiln.

[14] Philippians 1:21

Miss Byron then made the application that we are in God's hands and He is molding us into people who will worship Him and reflect His glory. "He is the Master Potter," she said. Though she directed her next words to the entire congregation, it was all about me that morning. "Remember," she said, "He bought us with the blood of His dear Son. He won't give up on us. We're just common clay, but in God's hands, well, there's no end to what He can do through us. Will you"—and I knew she said this to me—"allow Him to fashion you into a vessel that can carry His light into the dark places of the world?"

Yes, I would. I walked forward to dedicate my life for missionary work that Sunday morning. I was only nine years old but it was no flash-in-the-pan decision. Like my moment of salvation just months before, it would stand as a pivotal moment in my life's story. And with that thought, I fell asleep.

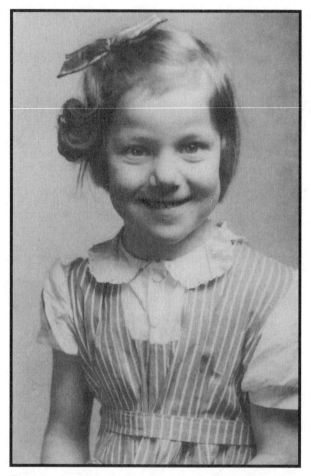

Grace Louise Jones at 7 years of age in Otego, New York.

⚡ CHAPTER NINE

Holy words

"There's a lovely Hasidic story of a rabbi who always told his people that if they studied the Torah, it would put Scripture on their hearts. One of them asked, 'Why on our hearts, and not in them?' The rabbi answered, 'Only God can put Scripture inside. But reading sacred text can put it on your hearts, and then when your hearts break, the holy words will fall inside.'"[15]

From that moment on I never looked at missionaries in the same way. *I could be one of them.* I sized them up. Obviously, the ones who helped with the dishes jumped to the top of my list. The ones who could speak another language also received high marks. I willingly gave up my bed for all of them.

I sat spellbound as they talked of people who worship idols, of people who had never heard the name of Jesus. When I touched the artifacts on their display tables, I felt both scared and thrilled. They somehow seemed sacred. The faces of people in missionary slides gripped me. It wasn't so much the rickshaws, or feather head-dresses but their faces—the skin tones, and different hair styles, but mostly the expressive eyes.

In high school I belonged to a High school Born-Againers Club and one of our assignments was to pray around the world. I took the project seriously, tacked a large world map above my bed, pasted

---

[15] Lamott, Anne. *Plan B*. New York: Penguin, 2005: 73.

requests and statistics all over it, then prayed. My grades in geography class improved dramatically, but more importantly, God quietly but surely laid a burden for the people of the world on the heart of this country girl.

My mother, an avid reader, discovered an organization called The Bible Memory Association. She soon had the family and members of the church involved in their memory system. During the cold New York winters our hearts were warmed by memorizing Scripture.

We propped the memory verse booklets above the sink so we could review as we washed dishes. Another dangled from the bathroom mirror. My mother pinned one page to the lace curtain beside the telephone, and she always kept a memory booklet in her apron pocket. It was not unusual to hear us mumbling verses to ourselves as we went about our household chores or waited for the school bus. I practiced mine again before I went to bed each night. In the morning I'd find the wrinkled booklet between the blankets or atilt on the floor. As a family and church we learned 20 verses a week for 12 weeks during each of my teen years.

While I diligently worked to earn the awards and a free week at camp, the Holy Spirit was at work encouraging me, nudging me to a deeper walk with Him. Psalm 23 says that He leads us in green pastures. I think David is talking about keeping our noses in the Word of God. I didn't realize it at the time, but I was, so to speak, stockpiling good truths—wholesome building blocks needed for constructing a life of spiritual qualities: discipline, loyalty and humility.

※

Many years after Martha Mai's death, my oldest sister Arloween was in the hospital. She needed a blood transfusion. A staff nurse failed to check her blood type carefully, and made the mistake of giving her a transfusion with the wrong blood type.

Was history repeating itself? First, Mommie died at 40 leaving five children. Now Arloween died at age 39, mother of five children ages 4-16. People told her husband and my father that such a blunder was unthinkable. "You should sue that hospital," they said. But my father replied, "No, we're not going to sue anyone; we will forgive."

It wasn't that Daddy felt no pain, or that forgiveness was easy, but he didn't want to carry resentment and negative feelings for the rest of his life. "This is the right thing to do," he said.

He demonstrated that pattern to us over and over through his ministry as pastor. One Sunday morning I lingered after the church service. I wanted to walk back to the parsonage with Daddy, my favorite person in the whole world. The line of parishioners shaking hands ended; others hurried home to put dinner on the table. "We better close the church windows," I called out.

My father remained alone in the foyer. He was crying. I went and stood quietly beside him wondering who could have hurt this dear man. "She (he didn't mention a name) didn't understand what I said. But it's okay," he said. We'll pray for her and forgive her, won't we?"

His model of forgiveness, lived out before us, became a significant cornerstone for my own life of faith. I can't say that I followed the pattern perfectly in my life but it has always echoed in my heart as a clear challenge.

How could I know that 24 years after Arloween's death my biggest test would come. In one decisive moment of my life, questions barged into my life. Who did it? Where were you, Lord? What do I do now? How do I cope? And this one, "What building blocks am I going to pass on to my children?" At least

I began that painful process with an advantage. Forgiveness was already woven into the fabric of my life by my father. He modeled it for me many times.

Then, that awful day in 1956. We sat glued to the radio, anxious for news of the five missionaries in Ecuador trying to reach the fierce Auca tribe. Others might consider me reckless but when I heard that five men had dared to go, I became more determined than ever to be a missionary.

Could He make a missionary out of shy, fearful clay?

Could I build my life on the Bible? Would it be a trustworthy building block in the midst of danger, reversals or tragedy?

How would forgiveness fit into the blueprint of my life?

What kind of structure would God make with the unique combination of building blocks passed down to me?

Decades later, when I revisited that church, some of the older members recalled in vivid detail the incident of Martha Mai's death. Then they described how they had reflected on my father's extension of forgiveness to the offender. "Our congregation was never the same after that."

That living object lesson not only impacted the congregation, but also became a significant building block for us children. Somewhat like King David[16], so long ago, who gave building materials to his son, Solomon, so he could build the temple, my father gave us children the sturdy building block of forgiveness we would need for life.

---

[16] 1 Chronicles 22

❧ CHAPTER TEN

Cut any cord

*"I took the road less traveled by,
and that has made all the difference."*[17]

In Genesis 22 we read the story of Abraham going up the mountain to sacrifice his son. Chills must have raced up his spine when Isaac asked, "Father, we have the fire and the wood, but where is the lamb?"

Those were the very verses my husband, Edmund and I read on July 2, 1969 in Brisbane, Australia. We were headed to our first missionary assignment as a married couple.

I had finished Bible College and linguistic training. I'd spent seven and a half years in southern Mexico working on the Huixteco translation project with Marion Cowan.

Then in 1967 when I returned to work on staff at one of our linguistic schools I met Edmund, a new missionary candidate. We fell in love and married that summer. But we hit a snag. The health officials in Australia quarantined us. "Didn't you know there was a cholera epidemic in Thailand?" they asked. We had spent a day in Thailand visiting the sights, taking a boat ride on the canal to see the floating market.

"No, we didn't know of any epidemic."

The nurses gave use cholera shots. Meanwhile our flight to Port Moresby, the capital of Papua New Guinea, departed without us

---

[17] Frost, Robert. "The Road Less Travelled." 1920.

and our luggage went to Tokyo! The good news? The airlines paid for our accommodation for two days until the next flight to Papua New Guinea.

Still wearing the grubby clothes we had traveled in from Germany, we visited a museum in Brisbane. It was full of stone axes, skulls, grotesque and, what I considered ugly, artifacts from New Guinea. Memory of my sister's recent death burned fresh in my mind. I felt nauseous at the sight of these museum pieces. Perhaps it had something to do with the fact that I was in my eighth month pregnant with our firstborn but I could see "death" written over all those artifacts.

In our hotel room that night I asked Edmund, "Are we really thinking of going to New Guinea? Are we crazy?"

A serious discussion followed.

"We could go back home, I guess," I stammered. "We could tell the director in Papua New Guinea that something came up and we couldn't make it."

"We could go and be missionaries in the nice neat country of Germany," Edmund added. We were hesitating, not so sure now about this thing labeled "God's call." It had seemed so easy back in the mission conferences in the U.S.A.

In spite of our jumbled thinking we paused to have our devotional time. Early in our marriage we had formed the habit of reading God's Word together before bedtime and so we turned to the next chapter listed on our Bible reading schedule—Genesis 22.

I started to read this familiar story. I came to verse 7, Isaac's question. "Father, we have the fire and the wood, but where is the lamb?" I stopped and looked at Edmund. Edmund looked at me. The shocking truth stabbed at both of our hearts at the same time. "We have the fire and the wood, don't we?" I said.

"We have our youthfulness and the finances," he added.

"And we have our training," I said.

"But the big question is do we have the lamb?" he said.

"It comes down to being willing to put our lives at risk, doesn't it?"

"It's not just the two of us. It's putting this little one on the altar too." I placed my hands on my fat belly.

"God has called us to this work. Do you still believe it, Grace?"

"Yes, I shouldn't let that museum visit distract me. We don't dare disobey God."

Edmund slipped down onto his knees beside the bed. We held hands as he prayed. That hotel room that evening became our Mt. Moriah. We rededicated our lives to the Lord. We knelt, it seemed, on holy ground. Graciously the Holy Spirit kept hidden from us that 25 years later to the day would be the date scheduled for the court case for Edmund's murder.

In Genesis 22, whether Isaac was to be the sacrifice or live a life of service does not seem to be the crux of the Abraham-Isaac story. The angel's response was, "Now I can see that you trust God and that you have not kept your son, your only son from me."

And so when Edmund died I had to go back to Brisbane in my mind and ask myself about my attitude. If in my heart I refuse to release Edmund to God, would God be able to say to me, "Now I see that you trust me because you have not withheld your loved one from me?"

No, He couldn't. If I become bitter or continually asked the question, "Why?" would that demonstrate my trust in God? I prayed again the prayer that I had written many years earlier in the flyleaf of my Bible:

"Lord, send me where Thou wilt,
Only go with me;

Lay on me what Thou wilt,
Only sustain me.
Cut any cord but the one that binds me
To Thy cause and to Thy heart."[18]

Edmund Fabian married Grace Jones on
August 25, 1967 after a summer romance.

---

[18] Livingstone, David

※ CHAPTER ELEVEN

Too late

"I now know that God has never been oblivious of one word I've spoken from the soul in His direction. The timing is His; the patience must be mine."[19]

From the moment we arrived in the mountainous area that is home territory to the Nabak people, we loved the mountains standing majestic and green and purple, always pointing heavenward. We loved the jungle-covered countryside, the slopes dotted with sweet potato gardens and the valleys between.

We loved the airstrip at Kasanombe. Sure, it is situated at a 14% incline but it saved us three to five days of tortuous hiking from the coast. A wrecked aircraft rests at the top end of the airstrip, aging and rusting. Appropriately, at the other end of the airstrip there is a cemetery. The airstrip is designated for a single-engine airplane. It is also designated as a "no-return" airstrip. That means that once a pilot starts his descent, he can't change his mind, circle and try again. There simply isn't room between the mountains. I guess you could say I was not exactly exuding with confidence when we landed there.

The village of Zinsaik, a half-hour's hike from the airstrip, where we chose to live, couldn't even earn a dot on the map but it was the largest of all the 53 Nabak hamlets that nestle peacefully here and there.

[19] MacDonald, Gordon. *The Life God Blesses.* Nashville: Thomas Nelson, 1997: 203.

On one side of "our" village dips a yawning gorge stretching down to the port town of Lae, 30 miles away as the crow flies. No roads penetrate this mountain wilderness, only rugged mountain trails, many of them narrower than the sole of your boot. The mountains seem packed together. We could hear a man yoo-hooing from one mountain to the next. But traveling that same distance took hours of scrambling down, down, down then up, up, up precipitous trails.

On the other side of our new home the damp rain forest is often wrapped in clouds. The heat and the ocean breezes at the coast send the clouds northward through the mountain ranges. Every morning we'd see the clouds chugging up the valley and staying all day. If I opened our front door they'd walk right in.

Here the Nabaks are born. Through rain and scorching sun they trek to the sweet potato gardens cultivating and digging their staple food. Here they live. Here they grow old and die. But not everyone grows old before dying. More than 50% of the population is younger than 18 years. Fifty-one out of a thousand children die before their fifth birthday.[20]

Three days after our arrival in Zinsaik we awoke in the middle of the night to the weird sounds of wailing and sobbing. We followed the haunting sounds to a nearby house. Shrouded women huddled around a lifeless body. Tears filled my eyes as I realized it was Maŋne. She was the wife of Gwakâp who worked at the agricultural station located near our translation support center at Ukarumpa.

---

[20] National Center for Health Statistics. <http://www.cdc.gov/nchs/data/dvs/LINK01WK46.pdf>.

Just the day before she had approached me, and using the trade language that she had picked up while with her husband at the agricultural station, she had told me a little bit about herself. She said that when her husband first got the job, she went to the agricultural station with him. But soon she grew homesick there and returned to her quiet Nabak village to be near her relatives. She went on to say that Gwakâp had urged her to come to the city for the birth of their third child. "I am afraid of the white man's hospital," she said. Then she added, "It is not our Nabak way to have strangers around at such a time. Just the opposite, we go to the banana grove, under the star-dotted sky and only one woman helps us."

Now she was gone. She died of retained placenta. She bled to death. I don't know if we could have helped her even if we had been asked. Maŋne would never know why we had come to Zinsaik to live. I had come too late for her. I sat with the women as they wailed. Inside I was wailing too.

Then they passed the wee baby girl to me. I felt honored that they would allow me to hold her.

When Edmund and I walked home in the moonlight, under the deep bluish-gray sky, I thought, "We're too late for Maŋne but maybe we're not too late for that little one."

Jonathan surrounded by Nabak children in 1971.

The butterfly pretty I see

People need the Lord,
People need the Lord;
At the end of broken dreams,
He's the open door.
People need the Lord,
People need the Lord;
When will we realize
People need the Lord.[21]

Sometime in the 16th century the Portuguese seafarer, Jorge de Meneses landed on the island of New Guinea and called it the Ilha dos Papuas, the island of the people with tightly curled hair.

In 1969, the same month that the first American landed on the moon, we also landed, not on Tranquility Base on the moon but on this far off island of Papua New Guinea.

We loved many things about living in Nabak land. What we didn't love was the fact that we couldn't understand a single word that the Nabaks spoke to us. They spoke continually but we did not share a single word in common. There were no textbooks or CDs to teach us the language.

The Nabak people themselves would be our teachers, but first they would have to satisfy their curiosity about us. They loved pulling

---

[21] TNelson, Greg and Phill McHugh. "People Need the Lord." River Oaks Music Co., 1983.

the hair on my arms. Their skin is smooth. Their hair is kinky, curly so they were intrigued by my straight hair. They called mine fur.

After just a few days I realized they had given me a name, "White person." How flattering is that?

We oohhed and ahhed over the wild orchids, cassowaries and birds of paradise. But it soon became obvious that we "white skins" were the most interesting things to show up in a long while. Though I am only 5' 3" tall, I am taller than most of the Nabak people. Since I was the first white woman that many of them had ever seen they pinched me and patted me all over to see if in fact I was a woman. Having lived with the shy, Mayan people of Mexico on my first linguistic assignment, this was definitely a crash course in cultural adjustment.

They lifted 4-month old Jonathan's shirt and exclaimed, "It's white under there too!" He was passed from one woman to another. If they hadn't seen him for a couple of hours they'd come to the house looking for him. They'd walk into the bedroom and pick him up. I didn't know enough of the language to tell them, "Hey, it took me two hours to get that child to sleep. Don't you dare wake him up."

When I walked around the village with Jonathan he was the center of attention, our P.R. man. They waved their hands right in front of his eyes delighting in his blue eyes blinking. We never had difficulty finding people to help us with the language when he was with us. One day when Jonathan was just starting to talk, he saw some wild flowers growing near one house. As usual, the women were sitting together making string bags and watching him. In his baby talk Jonathan reached for the flower and said, "Pawa, pawa." The women went wild, patting their breasts and shrieking, "He called us Pawa. He's already talking Nabak. He called us Pawa." Pawa is the Nabak word for "grandmother." I never did have the heart to tell them that he was really saying baby talk for "flower."

Before my marriage to Edmund I had lived in southern Mexico and learned Huixteco, a Mayan language. But Nabak, classified as a non-Austronesian language, seemed 50 times harder than Huixteco. The death of Maŋne gave us fresh impetus to hurry along in the language learning process.

And so began the painful process of pointing at objects hoping they would give us the Nabak word for that object. We wrote these words in phonetic script on 3x5 cards like they taught us at linguistic school.

In the evenings I sat beside our cast iron stove and alphabetized those cards and put them in a shoebox. I'm talking pre-computer days. Misery awaited anyone who tipped over the shoebox.

We papered our walls with newsprint and started writing down conjugations of verbs with their vast array of affixes. We finally figured out that the person markers and tense markers attached to the verb. Not separate words. The biggest problem, however, was that the verb changed its form each time a suffix was added. For instance, sometimes the verb meaning "go" looked like 'met'. But other times it might be 'med' or 'mel' or 'me' or 'be' or 'bet'. Why was it changing? It took some of the finest minds in Wycliffe to help us unravel the problem.

One day we overheard one of the village leaders explaining to the people the reason we were so slow to speak their language. He said, "They have hard heads and heavy mouths."

Some words were unpronounceable. The 'ŋ' sound occurs frequently—not just at the end of words like in the English word 'sing', but at the beginning and middle of words. For example 'his banana' is ŋaŋaŋ. It took practice to twist my tongue around these new combinations of sounds. Sometimes we missed final sounds because there was no puff of air like English words that end with a p, t, or k. Then there was that word 'to do' or 'to cause' which was simply "m".

My brain did gymnastics to reverse the English word order to fit the Nabak grammar. One day I managed to stammer out the sentence, "The butterfly pretty I see." It felt like a major accomplishment but I'm sure I sounded like a three-year old to the Nabak people.

Sweet potatoes are the basic food for the Nabaks. I had never seen so many varieties of sweet potato. One day I asked them to show me all the different kinds. They laid them out in some kind of scientific categories—thin ones to fatter ones, tan skins to red skins, hairy roots to long roots. By the end of the day we had 52 varieties of sweet potatoes. Then they proceeded to give me the Nabak word for each one—mâmeŋziŋ, mâeŋmaŋsat, mâŋwasute, mâseletak, mâtiki, mâwalia, mâwatut, moseletek... And I had 52 more Nabak words to add to our growing dictionary in the shoebox.

And wouldn't you know? Some eager man asked me for the name of each one in English. All I could say was, "sweet potato", "sweet potato", "sweet potato."

"English is very inadequate, isn't it?" he said.

I was forced to agree.

❦ CHAPTER THIRTEEN
Words wanted

O Lord, my Lord, I am a stranger in a strange land.
Absent are all the subtleties of custom and language and sight and smell
and taste which normally give me my bearings.
Jesus, everliving Teacher, use my out-of-placeness to remind me again of
my alien status in this world. I belong to another kingdom and live out
of another reality. May I always be ultimately concerned to learn the
nuances of this eternal reality so that when it becomes my permanent
residence I will not find it strange in the least.
In the name of him who entered a foreign land so that whosoever will
might come home to that for which they were created. Amen.[22]

Every day the number of cards in the shoebox grew. Some days I worried that if I shook my head, some of the new words I had just memorized would fall out.

One day someone's relatives came from the coastal town of Lae to visit. Their friend in the village brought them to our house to show us off. I greeted them with the typical Nabak greeting, "You've come." By this time we'd figured out that there were not just different singular and plural words for 'you' but a category of dual. I must have used the correct form.

"See," he said, "I told you. She speaks Nabak. And you wouldn't believe me."

---

[22] Foster, Richard. *Prayers from the Heart.* Quoted in Gire, Ken. *Reflections on the Word.* Colorado Springs: Chariot Victor, 1998: 205.

"One or two words only," I said, giggling with embarrassment. Then the visitor said, "I hear her. She's fluent."

Maybe our "heavy mouths" had lost a little weight, but "fluent"? Hardly. We weren't satisfied. I hadn't come 12,000 miles around the world to learn some exotic language so I could talk about sweet potatoes or butterflies. I wanted words to express ideas, things I couldn't point to or act out. I longed for words or phrases that conveyed grace, peace, hope.

So now we added a tape recorder to our linguistic paraphernalia. We recorded stories in village meetings or sitting around someone's fire pit. We needed a variety of stories. Would there be a different style if someone gave instructions on how to build a house? Is there a different way to introduce the topic if you're telling a personal experience, like my first ride in an airplane? Is there a different technique for telling traditional stories? We recorded hunting stories, village court sessions, jokes, and riddles. Zuke gave us the detailed procedure for building a house. It was from that text that we learned that the Nabaks have at least twenty different words to express the idea of 'carry'. They are differentiated semantically, according to how the object is carried: on top of the head, in one's arms, hanging from the shoulder, on one's back etc.

Then came the tedious task of transcribing the stories. The experts tell us that all languages are spoken at about the same rate but, of course, when you're learning a language it seems frightfully fast. That tape recorder got a workout as we paused, or rewound the cassette on almost every word. Gradually, with the help of Atak, Miliŋnâŋe and other patient men we parceled out each Nabak word, putting what we hoped was the correct definition underneath in English. These texts would become the basis of the grammatical analysis of the Nabak language.

Everyone wanted to tell a story to the little black machine so they could hear their voice back again. We had more than enough words. Nabak words swirled around us as everyone tried so hard to get them into our thick skulls. When we didn't get it right they would laugh and say it louder. If we still didn't get it right they increased their volume and their laughter. Our problem, though, was not because we were hard of hearing.

One day as Edmund sat in the house transcribing a text, I watched out the window as Jonathan played with a group of boys. They were making toy bows and arrows. "The three-pronged one is used for hunting birds," explained one of the boys.

"This smooth one's for killing pigs," said another.

"And see this? This sharp barbed one is for people. Yeah, this is for killing people," another piped up.

"How very reassuring is that," I thought.

I don't know what happened next but some quarrel erupted and one youngster started shouting, "Sakapitalak, come. Sakapitalak come." The boys scattered in all directions. I went out and brought Jonathan inside. Then I wrote down the new word 'sakapitalak' on a 3x5 card and showed the card to Edmund. He asked Atak, the young man, working with him about the meaning.

Atak was immediately concerned. "Where did you hear that word?"

"Oh, dear," I said to the men. "I hope I'm not collecting swear words." And I told about the quarrel in the front yard.

"Grandfather Leŋkepe can tell you all about sakapitalak. You need to ask him," Atak said.

That afternoon the old man came and told us the story. He wanted it recorded. "Sakapitalak is a white-skinned man with bushy hair all over his body. He wears a long beard and he's dirty and ugly. He eats bugs, grass and people…when he can get them. So that's why all the Nabak people are afraid of him."

I guess we didn't show enough fear so Leŋkepe continued in a whisper, "There are many sakapitalaks in the woods right behind your house. We haven't seen any in a long time but I thought you should know."

I made a mental note to tell Edmund never to grow a beard. Leave the bugs alone too, I thought.

Then Edmund asked, "How do you know what a sakapitalak looks like?"

"Well, you see, it was like this. One of our witchdoctors, a friend of mine, captured and killed a sakapitalak in the rainforest. He invited me and some of the other men to eat it. We offered half of the sakapitalak to the spirits. The other half we cooked and ate. All the other men who sat around the fire that day have since died. I am the only one left to tell this story. I saw it with my own eyes. I myself ate it. This is a true story."

This wasn't exactly what I had in mind when I set out in search of words. I couldn't shake away the idea that perhaps these Nabak men had eaten a Japanese soldier, a survivor of World War II. I will never know but Leŋkepe's story opened the window on a whole different worldview. They would experience the gospel through a specific cultural lens, an animistic perspective, vastly different from my own. Surely our presence among these people is out of this world. Did I really think that anyone would listen to my halting, inadequate explanation of the gospel? I knew, without a doubt, that if they did, it would be solely on the basis of the awesome grace of God, His outrageous grace.

⚂ CHAPTER FOURTEEN

looking through a straw

"Customs are quite different to what we've known. The one all absorbing idea in our lives is how to fit into God's plans and purposes for us. The Nabaks, instead, are dominated by the spirits. This belief penetrates every relation of life."[23]

Interpreting the language was only one segment of our lives among the Nabak people. Almost every day I saw behavior that I had difficulty fathoming its significance. I became painfully aware that I think and work on a different wavelength. It's as if I'd looked through the end of my straw and thought that what I saw was the only reality. Now I realized that others saw a completely different view through their straws. Would I be so proud as to think that what I saw through that tiny circle of my straw was the only truth? Or would I sit beside my new Nabak friends and ask them to tell me what they see through their straw?

Frankly, we were surprised at the confidence the people put in us. The old men considered it their forte to teach us their culture. One told us about using the gwasuta tree to work powerful magic to win a lover. "Go out to the jungle and cut a root from this tree. Each time the blade comes down call out the name of your girlfriend. Then take the root home and hang it over the fire.

---

[23] Quoting from my journal May, 1971.

When dance-singing season comes, burn the root and rub the ashes on the lizard skin of the drum. That night as you hit your drum for the dancing, it will have a different sound than all the other drums because the spirits will possess it. With each beat the drum echoes her name, just like when you chopped down the tree and called her name.

Soon the girl will look around, trying to figure out who called her. She will come and then you can tell her that you want to marry her."

When Edmund told me the story I reminded him that I had already heard him calling my name. He wouldn't need to resort to this.

We were sitting on the porch one evening talking with some Nabak friends when a little cluster of fireflies flitted nearby. Without the customary farewell, all of our friends ran off. They weren't running for a container to try and catch the fireflies. They believe that fireflies in a group is a sign that they are indwelled by a spirit and if one lands on you, you could burn up.

I was called to help a Nabak woman deliver her baby. She shivered in the rain in the banana grove. I begged her to come inside but she wouldn't. "The blood of childbirth causes asthma," she said.

Tâsioŋ was very upset because a rat gnawed on something in her house during the night. It wasn't because the rat had escaped from a trap and spoiled her favorite sweater. She believed the rat housed the spirit of her recently deceased baby and was scolding her for not feeding her enough.

Kwebok's father died in the garden. Relatives carried the corpse back home but Kwebok stayed at that spot. Why? To have some quiet time to grieve alone? No, he stayed to listen to what the gwapuput bird would tell him—murder or a natural death?

When Zeŋge arrived home after washing her clothes at the river, she realized her towel was missing. She retraced her steps but could not find it. I suggested that one of the other women had mistakenly picked it up. She woke up that night, "The water spirits pulled my towel into the water and now they're pulling me in." The next morning she went to the river and tried to drown herself. Her uncle, working in his garden on the other side of the river, saw what was happening and rescued her.

"The thief comes only to steal and kill and destroy; I have come that they may have life, and have it to the full."[24]

---

[24] John 10:10

Edmund built a water piping system for the Zinsaik village. Before, the closest water source was a stream a 20 minute hike down and up a steep hill. With this plumbing system the people could get water out of two faucets in the center of the village.

Edmund, whose main job was working on the translation also practiced his nursing skills. This pregnant lady's baby being forced out by a relative, causing much tearing and bleeding to the mother, became the worst medical case witnessed. She is being carried from the Fabian house to the airstrip to catch a small plane to a hospital in the coastal town of Lae.

🎜 CHAPTER FIFTEEN

The choice

Do you not know—
That our lives—
Both yours and mine—
Are woven into one
By countless fragile threads—
Of different colored dreams—
And some are of the flames
And some are of the ashes—
Beside this murky pond—
I saw the Alchemist at work.[25]

Just a thread of gold and crimson remained in the sky as the sun dropped behind the mountains. That's when I heard a gentle cough at the door of our house in the remote village where we lived in Papua New Guinea. A cough is the Nabak custom for knocking. I opened the door to see one of my Nabak neighbors standing outside. Lines of worry and fear creased her face. She thrust her baby into my arms.

Edmund, a male nurse, grabbed his stethoscope, then examined the baby. "Pneumonia, and he's badly dehydrated." He started with a dropper to press liquids and antibiotics through the baby's lips.

---

[25] Abbott, Winston. *O. Come Climb My Hill.* South Windsor, CT: Inspiration House, 1988: 42-43.

I stoked the fire in our cast iron stove. It would be a long night. While the coffee perked, I padded into our son's bedroom and found a baby blanket. Edmund wrapped up the little patient in it, then sat in front of the stove cuddling him.

As Edmund nursed this fragile baby back from death's door, I prayed, "Lord, lay your healing touch on this precious little one. Keep him alive. You've brought these people here; help us to show them your love."

I told the mama that if we could keep her baby alive until morning, we would arrange for an airplane to come. "You will need to go to the hospital in town. They have better facilities there. Your baby will receive good treatment there."

The mama, when she saw the loving care Edmund gave her baby, relaxed, stretched out on the floor and dozed off. Edmund and I took turns all through the night dropping or spooning liquids into the baby's feverish body.

At the crack of dawn, I had difficulty thinking of anything except my warm, cozy bed. I was almost afraid to look at Edmund and the baby. His mother still slept on the floor. "I think there's a bit more color in his cheeks," I whispered.

"You're just hoping that," Edmund said. "He still clings to life by a thread."

"At least he's alive," I said.

"If only they hadn't waited four days before bringing him…" He stopped in midsentence. Fatigue edged into his words as he handed the baby to me.

I woke up the mama, gave her a cup of coffee and a biscuit. While she ate I told her, "Gather some clothes and diapers to take to the hospital in town. Come back here before you go to the airstrip. I'll write a letter that you can give to the doctor."

As I fairly shoved them out the door I repeated, "Come back here for the letter, okay?"

I turned and dashed to the two-way radio, our only contact with the outside world. "Alfa Foxtrot, Alfa Foxtrot, we have an emergency. Over." Between the crackles and static I made flight arrangements.

"Good news, Edmund, they are coming," I said.

Then I started typing the letter of referral. The mother didn't know a word of the trade language, and I knew it would be very frustrating for her and for the doctor without my explanation.

While my sleep-deprived brain composed the letter, I kept glancing out the window to see if the mother and baby were returning. They weren't. *How long does it take to grab some diapers and stuff them into a net bag? Has she misunderstood and gone straight to the airstrip?*

Satisfied with the wording of my letter, I asked Edmund to sign his name with an R.N. then I tucked it into an envelope. I expected to hear the drone of an airplane any minute now. I knew the hospital plane always sat ready at the airport at the coast. In fifteen minutes he'd poke through the clouds and circle to make sure no people wandered onto the strip. Then he'd make his landing.

I looked out the window again, looking east for an approaching dot in the sky. Then I checked in the other direction for the mother and her sick baby. No plane. No mama.

"Why isn't she rushing over?" I asked Edmund. But he was headed to the bedroom to take a quick nap before the translation team arrived.

"Don't worry. I'm sure she'll be here in a minute or two," he said and staggered away.

Concerned that the patient wouldn't be at the airstrip when the plane arrived, I decided to race over to her house. *I must explain the plan more carefully this time.* I certainly hadn't reached the "fluent-in-Nabak" level yet. We'd only been studying Nabak for 15 months.

There she sat cross-legged on her verandah, her right hand flying with the thread as she crafted a string bag. The listless baby lay across her lap.

Taken aback by her nonchalant pose, it took me a minute to compose my thoughts. "Uhh, the plane is coming," I finally managed. "I contacted the hospital on the radio and they said they'd be here in a few minutes. Oh, there it is right now." I pointed down the valley.

Silence. *She doesn't get it. I'm sure I used the correct words, proper Nabak grammar. What's the problem?*

I took a deep breath and started again. "Here's the letter for the doctor. Have you packed your bag? You really need to get to the airstrip...uhh soon, like right now."

"I'll let him be buried here," she said.

Had I heard right? "Wha...what did you say?

"I said I'll let him be buried here."

My body went limp. I gulped, sick in the pit of my stomach. I had come to Papua New Guinea in obedience to a call God gave me. I wanted to enrich people's lives by translating the Word of God for them, and living out the gospel before them. I hadn't counted on them choosing death when I offered life.

❦ CHAPTER SIXTEEN

The red knot

*"When we return to this land,
you must tie this red rope
in the window through which you let us down.
Rahab answered, 'I agree to this.'
So she sent them away, and they left.
Then she tied the red rope in the window."*[26]

When evangelists first hiked from their coastal village to the mountains of Papua New Guinea in the early 1900s they wondered how they could express the gospel to a group of Nabak-speaking people who lived there. They had heard the message of salvation from German missionaries who had settled in their coastal villages. Now they were eager to go inland and spread the good news. But they faced a language barrier. They decided to try an object lesson.

After a strenuous three-day hike, they arrived at a settlement of Nabak people. Foreigners are never welcomed warmly. At least they had the same skin color and kinky hair. Finally the Nabak leaders, all elderly men, agreed to meet with these strangers.

The evangelists held up strips of red cloth, and using the trade language they explained as best they could, "The red represents the blood of Jesus that he shed when he died on the cross for our sin."

---

[26] Joshua 2:18, 21

With more gestures and repetition they started tying the strips of cloth to their wrists and to the wrists of the Nabak people.

Up to this point the Nabak elders sat quietly observing. But now they leaned forward, scrutinizing the foreigners as they tied the knot. "Just like we two are joined together, God wants to join himself and us people on the ground," the leader of the evangelist said.

"It's picture talk," another evangelist said. He put his arm next to the arm of a Nabak man and with his other hand tied a knot in the red cloth. "See, now we're together. That's what God wants to do."

The Nabak chief signaled to the other men. In an instant the Nabak men knew that their plan to kill these evangelists was off. They assigned the foreigners a place to sleep, though earlier they had said that the visitors would not be allowed to stay overnight.

While they slept, the Nabak elders met in the men's house, a special longhouse in the middle of the village where all major decisions were made. The initiation ceremonies for all the young men coming of age took place in the men's house. No woman was ever allowed to enter. As the men squatted before the fire pit to warm their hands, the leading elder began. "I know we agreed this morning, when we saw those foreigners coming over the mountain, that we would trick them into sitting down and talking," he said.

"Then we'd surprise them and kill them," said another.

"We saw your signal and figured you must have something else in mind. What was that knot anyway?" said another.

They looked around into each other's faces. No one had seen a knot like that. "It's different. Not at all like the kind of knots we make."

"This is a new knot. Our ancestors never taught us that one."

That night the men agreed that the knot held some kind of uniqueness. Before going to sleep they all agreed on three things.

First, they would invite the foreigners to have another meeting in the morning so they could better discern their words. "Second, everyone must pay very close attention to the knot," the chief said. And, third, they decided to call the entire village to come and hear what the evangelists said. "Everyone should see those knots in the red cloth," the leading elder said.

"It was because of that knotted cloth," the Nabaks told me later, "that we listened to the messengers and did not harm them."

The Nabak people have a custom related to tying knots. It is their way of pointing out or marking an item. It indicates that a promise or agreement has been made. For instance, if any passerby sees a vine from the leaf of wild sugar cane knotted on a string of bananas, he knows it's designated by the owner as a gift to an uncle, or for a feast.

Exchange relationships are very common among the Nabaks. If a man gives a butchered pig to someone as a gift, he lays a knot made from tough vine on top of the pig meat. Later, when the one who received the pork wants to give a gift back to that person, he returns the vine with his gift. But now he unties the vine. It's almost as if he says, "Look, we've got a relationship going here. You started it, now I'm doing my part." It's a symbol of mutual trust and unity.

The Nabak people also do very intricate string art. It's a complicated form of cat's cradle. Some make complex designs by holding the string in their fingers, their teeth and their toes.

Or sometimes a group of women performs the design together. They form a circle and each holds onto the string that has been tied to form a circle. As the women dance and sing they move to pick up a section of the string from someone else. Following the rhythm of the song, one after another they duck and lunge. The string criss-crosses the circle and at first looks like a mingled mass, but suddenly a bird-of-paradise shape appears. As the ladies step back and forth the wings of the bird flap.

Of all the object lessons that the evangelists might have used to explain the gospel, they chose the perfect one that resonated with the Nabak people. And so, before we arrived on Christmas day, in 1969, God had already been at work preparing Nabak hearts, using a knot, of all things.

As we helped the Nabak translate the words of the living God into their mother tongue, we came across the word "agreement" or "covenant" many times. After much discussion, we chose the word "knot" to represent this truth. God tied his knot with the Nabak. His words in the New Testament are called "God's new knot." Blessed be the tie that binds.

⚅ CHAPTER SEVENTEEN
One blood, one name

"Everyone must learn to believe in someone or something so deeply that life is charged with meaning and a sense of mission. And the more one dedicates oneself to this meaning and mission, the more such a person will develop a sense of profound and personal belonging and discover the reality of community."[27]

In 1972 we returned to our translation support center to await the birth of our second child. At the same time a young Nabak man, Zumbek, begged to please help with this language project. We decided he would make a good contribution to our linguistic project, so we took him along.

I did give birth to a beautiful baby girl. We named her Dietlinde, a German name meaning "strong linden tree". We loved her doll-like features and long black hair. There was little time to cradle her or to admire her fingers, because after a normal delivery complications set in. It was confusing to see two of our missionary pilots talking with the doctor. "The moon isn't out," I overheard as they whispered together in the corner.

Then they brought a stretcher and pressed it underneath me and carried me to a waiting van. I, like Maŋne, had retained placenta and was slowly bleeding to death. The doctor had hoped I could go to the government hospital by plane, but with no moonlight it was impossible to fly one of our single engine planes.

[27] Powell, John. *Fully Human, Fully Alive*. Niles, IL: Argus, 1976: 23.

I would go the seventy-five miles on a winding, pot-holed road, stretched out in the back of the van. A doctor crouched on one side of me, a nurse knelt on the other. Edmund sat in the front seat holding the newborn, worried that he would soon be a single parent.

All the time, I received fluids intravenously. My blood pressure plummeted. Several times we stopped beside the road to let the doctor vomit. He got carsick facing backwards. I tried to lighten the tenseness in the air by joking. "Hey, I thought I was the sick one."

I started to fade in and out of consciousness. When Edmund reached behind the seat to touch my head, I guessed I was dying. "Is there anything we need to talk about?" he said.

"Take care of Jonathan and Dietlinde for me," I told him, then faded into unconsciousness again.

The van slid around one tight corner after another. As we fishtailed, I slid from one side of the stretcher to the other. Ada, the nurse, held my hand and made sure the intravenous stayed secure. Periodically, Dr. Stan checked my pulse and blood pressure, which dropped dangerously low.

I felt alone in the darkness but I wasn't afraid. Though the other passengers were dear friends, and doing their best for me, I knew whatever happened it was God who had the final say. Prayers ascended. It's okay to be in the dark with God. His presence makes all the difference.

Then I felt a big, wet glob slide between my legs. It was a different movement than blood soaking into my pad. "The placenta has come. I'm sure the placenta has come," I said. "We don't have to go to the hospital."

By the light of a flashlight the doctor and nurse examined me. The driver, one of my Wycliffe associates, would have been quite happy, I'm sure, to not have to make the rest of the trip. Traveling on this mountainous road by day was difficult enough. Maneuvering these curves on a rainy, foggy night was strenuous and dangerous. He slowed momentarily. "Keep going," the doctor said. "Keep going."

I was barely alive when we arrived three hours later at the government hospital in Goroka. An Australian doctor examined me and said my blood pressure was down to 67. That's when I learned that I had not passed the placenta but a huge clot of blood.

Before operating, the doctor gave me two pints of blood. It felt like someone had opened a window to the cool, ocean breezes on a stifling hot day.

Before the ordeal was over, I required six pints of blood. Every drop of blood in those transfusions came from Papua New Guineans.

Since arriving on this island of New Guinea, I had prayed that somehow I would fit in. Now a new prayer rose in my heart. "Lord, their blood is flowing through my veins. I have become one with them in my body. Now please help me to become one with them in my thinking, in my spirit, so I can more adequately share your wonderful gospel with them."

As I began to regain strength I commented to the nurses how good the hospital food was. She said, "Too bad that man in the room next door isn't as sick as you were. He's done nothing but complain." Edmund and I could do nothing but rejoice in God's kindness to us. Wasn't it outrageous grace that had spared my life?

Back at our linguistic center, Zumbek and Edmund did most of the housework. Kind neighbors brought in food. Before long we picked up the linguistic studies again. Two months after Dietlinde's birth, Edmund and Zumbek finished an abridgement of the first eleven chapters of Genesis.

In spare minutes between caring for a new baby and her big brother, I studied more about Nabak customs. Zumbek clued me in to an aspect of the Nabak culture that I hadn't grasped before. He said that they don't normally call each other by their given names. Instead, they most commonly use their birth order. For example, every firstborn son of anyone in the village has the name '*Ayu*'. A second-born son is '*Amuŋ*'. A third-born son is '*Angwat*'. And the list goes on.[28] There's a separate list for women, '*Mâ*', '*Wene*', '*Tâ*', and on for a total of nine. I told Zumbek I had three older sisters. Zumbek immediately figured I was the fourth-born daughter and said, "Your Nabak name is '*Dambi*'.

" '*Dambi*' is definitely an improvement over 'White Woman' ", I said. None of them had even attempted to pronounce my real name, Grace, because there is no 'gr' sequence in the Nabak language; and no words ending in the 's' sound. Probably if they tried, it would come out something like 'gui-lacy'.

Even though the birth order names don't seem to imply affection, I felt positively heady when Zumbek started calling me '*Dambi*'. I knew it wouldn't take the people back in the village long to catch on to this new name. Was I really becoming a legitimate member of Nabak society? I certainly hoped so.

---

[28] Interestingly, the words *yu, mu, gwat* also mean index finger, middle finger, ring finger. They also form the lexical items for the different days of the week: *beyu* means Thursday, *bebmu* means Wednesday and *begwat* means Tuesday.

⚅ CHAPTER EIGHTEEN

Your inner being

"Sometimes,
like a mighty river
that thunders and echoes
through weathered canyon walls,
Your Word floods my soul, Lord,
surging in with power to cleanse away debris."[29]

Some of our language studies with Zumbek were absolutely boring for him as a teen-ager, who had dropped out of school. Playing marbles had to be more fun, but he stuck with us. For relaxation he entertained Jonathan.

We were dead serious about, do I dare say it, consonants. Yes, consonants. How could we hope to translate God's Book if we couldn't write the language's consonants accurately? And how could we teach the Nabak people to read and write until we uncovered the patterns of the sound system?

Every language originated in the mind of God, so we prayed that God would help us figure out the design of Nabak. Using those cards in the shoebox, Zumbek's keen mind and big doses of insight from our brilliant colleagues, we listed multiple contrasts of the Nabak consonants. For example: *tip, dip, sip, zip, mip, nip, kwip.* If we

---

[29] Goss, Geraldine A., *Sometimes*. Quoted in Morgan, Richard L. *Remembering Your Story*. Nashville: Upper Room, 2002: 49.

could find all the contrasts we'd know how many consonants there were in Nabak. Nabak had no previous orthography so it was our job to postulate what the sound system of Nabak was all about. We discovered Nabak had six vowels as in *sit, set, sat, sât, sot, sut,* and sixteen consonants.

Repeating Nabak words into an oscilloscope, a voice detection machine, and looking at the speech wave flowing across the page, intrigued Zumbek and us. Through the timing of the wave, we learned that the combination of sounds we originally posited as one syllable was actually two. Slowly we gathered the data to devise a scientific alphabet.

What Zumbek enjoyed the most was helping us translate our stories into Nabak. Edmund and Zumbek spent hours with their heads together. Zumbek wanted to hear Edmund's Poland story. Edmund happily told him what an anchor his mother's strong faith had provided in those horrible times. "Those war experiences prepared my heart so that when I heard the gospel at sixteen years of age, I was open to it," he said. They translated that sentence into Nabak using our tentative alphabet.

Then Edmund continued. "One Sunday night I saw a movie depicting the life of Martin Luther." Zumbek knew the name well. Wasn't it the national evangelists in the Lutheran church on the coast who had first reached into the Nabak area with the red knot object lesson? Since then many Lutheran churches dotted the area. Zumbek had been through the catechism classes and had become a member of the Lutheran Church in his village. But the gospel had come in the dress of a coastal language, not his heart language, Nabak. Some of the older people who had the privilege of attending school where the coastal language was taught, grasped the rudimentary aspects of the Christian teaching. But that school had closed, so for Zumbek's generation, being a follower of Christ meant little more than a certain ritual, a Sunday morning obligation. *When will the gospel filter past this superficial layer and reach deep into their core assumptions?*

Phrase by phrase, Zumbek turned Edmund's testimony into Nabak. "After that movie, I felt such keen conviction of my sin that I walked behind the church and cried. It took a visiting preacher to my usually liberal-leaning church to explain to me what I could do about my sin."

Then Edmund told Zumbek that when he rode his bike to school the next day, it was like a fight going on in his heart. He stopped in the ditch beside the road, knelt down and prayed, "All right, Lord, I give myself completely to You."

Using a local analogy Zumbek would understand, Edmund said, "It was like a heavy net bag dropped off me. I sang as I rode the rest of the way to school. I even stopped a few more times to pray. After school, I went straight home and found the Bible the teacher gave me at my confirmation. Suddenly I wanted to read it. It made sense to me."

As Zumbek and Edmund worked hand-in-glove crafting the words into Nabak, a mysterious yearning flooded Zumbek's inner being. *I don't know anything about this joy. I've never talked to God about my sin.*

Edmund practiced the sentences of his Nabak testimony over and over in front of Zumbek and me, refining his pronunciation. As he grew more fluent, Zumbek would jump in with an idea to make the story more compelling. "Don't say a fight was going on in your heart. That doesn't make sense to me. Say a fight was going on in your insides, in your inner being."

A few days later, Zumbek told us that he had seen an announcement on the post office board inviting people to sign up for a trip to the highlands town of Goroka. Ralph Bell of the Billy Graham Association was holding a five-day preaching crusade. Zumbek signed up.

The morning after the big meeting Zumbek came to the translation office, his face aglow. "I went forward," he said. "I did what you told me you did in Germany. I talked to God about my sin. I asked Jesus to become the big man of my life. I know now what you meant when you talked about that heavy net bag dropping off."

Back in the village, Zumbek told his family, "When Mr. Bell asked if anyone wanted to turn from their sin, I couldn't sit any longer on the chair. I heard some sort of voice saying that this is your time. Now go to the front. The words from God's Book were shooting into my insides like an arrow."

The testimony of the life of one great man of God, Martin Luther, challenged another man to bow before the God of grace. Now, Edmund's testimony and the preaching of Ralph Bell influenced another young man to follow the path of God's amazing, outrageous grace.

Not many days later Zumbek told us that he would like very much to go to Bible College. He suggested that his cousin Kondo would be a good person to take his place at the translation desk.

Our furlough would begin in July of that year so it seemed a good idea. We would sponsor Zumbek at Christian Leaders' Training College where he could grow in his newfound faith. We'd give Kondo the carbon copies of our first draft of translation to look over while we were away; we would go on furlough to show off our two children, show pictures of the Nabak people and ask for prayer help for our second term.

❧ CHAPTER NINETEEN

Sweet fragrance, flapping loincloth

"…There is a similarity between Christianity and animism in that they are both power religions. Christianity believes in the power of God. Animism believes in the power of spirit-beings. Knowing this, the missionary has abundant material in the Bible to speak to animists about the power of the Creator God and the power of Jesus."[30]

Zumbek was right. Kondo met the requirements of an ideal co-translator. He had an uncanny way of explaining the complications of the Nabak grammar. He mentored us in awkward cross-cultural situations. Most importantly, he ran a close second to being as patient as Job with our fumbling understanding of Nabak.

We transitioned, from translating short stories for literacy booklets, to the Gospel of Mark. Edmund and I practiced division of labor. He sat with Kondo and translated. I sat with Jonathan and Dietlinde typing the handwritten translation. Little arrows and squiggly lines directed me to the side or back of the page. It would have been easier to find my way through a cornfield maze.

We exchanged pages at the end of the day. Edmund received my neatly typed ones. I ended up with the scribbles of Nabak words. Every time Edmund and Kondo edited, I either had to retype the full page or cut and glue sections together. I became very proficient with the glue bottle.

[30] Blaschke, Robert C. *Quest for Power.* Ontario: Guardian Books, 2001: 26.

I'm sure computers were invented specifically with Bible translators in mind. Pure joy, when Edmund could sit in front of his computer screen and insert his own corrections, edit, revise, cut and paste, whatever. Good-bye to the shoebox. Good-bye to the portable typewriter. Not a single regret or thought for the "good ol' days" in my mind. How could translation be so much fun?

The test for how well we translated came one night around midnight. Kondo's wife woke up screaming hysterically, "The water spirits! Help, the water spirits." Specks of perspiration covered her forehead. "They're pulling me into the water," she gasped, finding it hard to breathe. Her eyes darkened with fear. Some formidable force pushed toward her. "Help, I'm drowning!"

Noting the fear in her voice, Kondo ran over to the office and picked up the pages of the newly translated Gospel of Mark. He helped Zeŋge into a sitting position and started reading passage after passage of how this very powerful Jesus chased out the evil spirits from people.

A man was there who had an evil spirit in him…Jesus commanded the evil spirit, "Be quiet!" The evil spirit shook the man violently, gave a loud cry, and then came out of him.[31]

Kondo turned the page and kept reading.

When Jesus got out of the boat, instantly a man with an evil spirit came to him from the burial caves…The demons begged Jesus, "Send us into the pigs; let us go into them." So Jesus allowed them to do this. The evil spirits left the man and went into the pigs.[32]

Zeŋge's breathing was quiet now. She shifted her position, not wanting to miss a word of Kondo's reading.

A woman whose daughter had an evil spirit in her…begged Jesus to force the demon out of her daughter…The woman went home and found her daughter lying in bed; the demon was gone."[33]

---

[31] Mark 1:23-25
[32] Mark 5:2-12
[33] Mark 7:25-30

Zeŋge's nightmare began to fade from her eyes. "Is this what you and the white man have been turning into our talk?"

"Yes, exactly these words. They are powerful words, true?" Leafing through the pages Kondo said, "I want to read you one more story."

Strange, but peaceful thoughts replaced the chill of the dark images as Kondo read.

"Teacher, I brought my son to you. He has an evil spirit in him and that stops him from talking. When the spirit attacks him, it throws him on the ground. Then my son foams at the mouth grinds his teeth, and becomes very stiff"...As soon as the evil spirit saw Jesus, it made the boy lose control of himself, and he fell down and rolled on the ground, foaming at the mouth...Jesus ordered the evil spirit... "You spirit that makes people unable to hear or speak, I command you to come out of this boy and never enter him again!" The evil spirit screamed and...came out. "[34]

Kondo laid the sheaf of papers aside, bowed his head and prayed for Zeŋge. She rolled over and went back to sleep, sleeping peacefully the rest of the night.

From that day forward, Kondo knew with absolute assurance that his job at the translation desk was infused with hope for his people. He said he felt called to this work as much as we did. We never doubted it.

But it wasn't a vocation for the fainthearted. We finished the four Gospels and the Acts of the Apostles. The Epistles, well, that seemed beyond us. I remember clearly one of the last translation checking sessions with Kondo. We discussed Colossians 2:15. In that verse it talks about Christ making a "public spectacle" of Satan when he died on the cross. *"Public spectacle," how do you say that in Nabak?*

We set it aside and moved to 2 Corinthians. We hit a snag at chapter 2 verse 14. I wondered how we could ever express these

---

[34] Mark 9:17-27

concepts in the Nabak language. The scene is a triumphal procession of Paul's day accompanied by the sweet odors from the burning of spices in the streets. Then we talked about the cinnamon bark that the Nabaks burn to give a pungent aroma during their dancing, and how our lives are a fragrance to the Lord and to others around us because the Good News is within us.

At last, we were satisfied that we had stated these verses in Corinthians clearly at least, it was the best we could do for now. It was time for coffee break and Kondo stepped outside to stretch. He noticed the rose bushes growing next to the office wall, lovingly planted and cared for by my husband, and now budding and blooming. "That's the way we are most of the time," he commented.

I wasn't sure what he meant but he continued, "The rose has a beautiful fragrance, but no one knows it until the rose blooms. Most often we Christians stay tightly closed like these buds." He held a bud gently between his fingers as he continued. "We often keep the Good News to ourselves, but the verses we translated today are telling us to open up and let the fragrance of Christ come out."

In the afternoon we continued. "Sweet aroma" was one thing, but what about "triumphal procession?"

We talked about the humiliation the conquered people would feel as they are led through the crowds of cheering victors and presented to the king.

To my surprise Kondo said, "This isn't a problem to translate. We do almost the same as Bible times." He described a traditional song and dance that the Nabaks enjoyed performing as their victorious warriors came home from battle. He even demonstrated how the victors flap their loincloth in the faces of their defeated foes to humiliate them and we realized that we had the expression we needed for that other troublesome verse in Colossians about "public spectacle."

So, in Nabak we say, "When Jesus died on the cross he took away the bow and arrows from Satan. Jesus disarmed him, and, in a manner of speaking, He flapped His loincloth in their faces."

I've thought of those beautiful words so often since Kondo's death in 1987. What a powerful word for a people who for centuries lived in fear of the spirits. "We don't need to be afraid of the spirits, do we? They were soundly defeated at the cross," they said.

After twelve years, very fruitful years, of working with us on the Nabak New Testament, Kondo was diagnosed with liver cancer. A week later he bled to death in the hospital as the doctor took a biopsy of his liver. His beloved translation lay on the pillow beside him.

During his short life he wrote 152 hymns. He taught us many of the intricacies of the language and its grammar. He was our mentor in cross-cultural issues. He was one of the first to understand the power of the gospel over the spirits. At the funeral Edmund told the story of the roses blooming. "Kondo was my best friend in all the world. Indeed, he blossomed and left a sweet aroma of God's presence in all of our hearts."

Kondo, on left, our faithful co-translator for 12 years with Zeŋge and his young family.

❦ CHAPTER TWENTY

A piece of chocolate cake

"The cords of death entangled me;
the torrents of destruction overwhelmed me.
The cords of the grave coiled around me.
The snares of death confronted me."[35]

W e wondered how we could possibly carry on without Kondo alongside to cheer us, without his keen mind to wrestle with the key terms. It was my husband's remarkable dedication (some called it stubbornness) and the amazing grace of God that kept us plowing ahead. Using other dedicated Nabak men and women for uncertain periods of time, we inched ahead verse by verse.

Finally in 1993 our translation to-do list grew shorter and we could actually imagine seeing the end of this huge project. Since our twins, Heidi and Kurt, would soon be graduating from high school in Papua New Guinea, we decided to double our efforts to make sure the translation was completed before they left the country. That's when I made my announcement at breakfast, "God is in His heaven, all is right with the Fabian world."

Now, just five years after losing Kondo from our team, Edmund had been torn from us. *So much for doubling our efforts.* I felt lightheaded and nauseous. My mind whirled with fear and sadness and despair—fear for my own life, sadness that my children were fatherless, despair that

---

[35] Psalm 18:4-6

the key figure in our translation program was wiped out by the swift blade of an axe.

I was so glad to have Zumbek nearby. I needed his friendship and his knowledge of the culture during this time of excruciating emotional pain. He would have to return to his teaching job soon and he said he wanted to make another trip to Kainantu to visit Miliŋnâŋe in jail.

Just as Zumbek stepped out the door I had an idea. "Oh, wait a minute," I said. "Look, people have brought us food and there's more than we can possibly eat. Here, take this chocolate cake to Miliŋnâŋe. He'll be hungry."

A few hours later Zumbek returned and I quietly asked him, "How is Miliŋnâŋe?"

"He's trembling and can't raise his head," Zumbek said.

"Did you give him the cake," I asked?

"Yes, but it was too heavy so I put one piece in his hand. Then I walked around the cell giving each of the others a piece. When I came back to Miliŋnâŋe he just stood there looking at the cake in his hand so I said, 'You can eat it. Grace thought you would be hungry so she sent it over with me.'

"Then Miliŋnâŋe said, 'I can't eat it. This is holy food; it comes from Grace. It is too sacred for my lips.' "

When Zumbek related this story to me I felt a rush of pity for this man. For the first time I realized that my children and I weren't the only ones suffering. This man, the perpetrator of the crime, was also in anguish.

I would, no doubt, receive sympathy and compassion from everyone who heard about my husband's murder but Miliŋnâŋe would be shunned. He would live with heavy guilt and the consequences of his actions all his life.

Just that day the country's newspaper, The Post Courier, carried the news of Edmund's death "Missionary axed to death". The words took my breath away.

That afternoon a very somber group of Nabak leaders arrived at my house. Each one spoke in turn expressing their regrets for what had happened. In the Nabak culture, this was not just an act by one individual, but the community held responsibility. This had brought shame to their society and particularly to the Sanau clan of which Miliŋnâŋe was a member.

I listened to their well-thought-out speeches then served them food. I gathered Miliŋnâŋe's belongings and gave them to his relative, along with Miliŋnâŋe's pay for his fortnight of work. Then the phone rang. Our office had received word that Miliŋnâŋe and another prisoner had escaped from jail. The Nabak delegation couldn't believe it.

"He doesn't know his way around the area."

"He could never find his way home," said another.

They agreed, "He's gone out of his mind."

They hurried to leave. I shook hands with each one and thanked them for coming.

No sooner had I shut the door than two other men came. "We've heard the news of the escapee. We're worried that he might come back here and kill you, so we're going to be guarding your house tonight."

I couldn't explain to anyone why I felt safe. Anything I said would sound naïve. Hadn't I felt safe last week Thursday when Edmund was killed in this very house?

The next day we learned that it was all a mistake. No one had escaped. The guard hadn't counted right.

I was too occupied with planning a funeral and choosing a burial site to reflect on the visit of the Nabak delegation or the miscount.

The phone rang constantly. Information was needed for press releases in America, England, Australia. Suddenly I was a celebrity. The American Embassy wanted to help and I told them about Dietlinde's expired passport. They said they would take care of it. Someone said that a friend of theirs was writing a book and wanted to include my story. Would I write a few paragraphs for him?

I had a long list of people who needed to be notified of Edmund's death. Composing a newsletter any time is a challenge for me but with these circumstances and on short notice, it was a major undertaking. I also needed a German translator for correct information to be sent to Edmund's family.

I pushed aside grief and filled in forms for life insurance, death certificate, workers' compensation, Social Security and bank accounts. My new status as widow required a change of my employee number. I loathed one more change.

Through the loops and tangles of this tragedy, I never forgot the words Miliŋnâŋe spoke after receiving the cake. How could I know that when I offered a chocolate cake to my husband's murderer I would be moving into new territory. What I discovered about God, myself and life as I traveled ahead, turned out to be filled with grace. Outrageous grace.

For now, I was happy to hear that Jonathan and Dietlinde were on their way. Was it only four months ago that we laughed together and celebrated Jonathan and Amy's wedding?

※ CHAPTER TWENTY–ONE

The upper hand

"We were knocked down, but we didn't remain there.
We kept popping back up.
Just as the sand in the bottom of the punching bag
constantly righted it,
so the truth of the Word of God kept us grounded
and stabilized so that we could not remain defeated by death's vicious blows" [36]

It slowly sank in that the cake I had given to Miliŋnâŋe had much greater significance than I could have imagined. My spontaneous act of kindness turned out to be a baby step toward forgiveness. Would I find the strength for the next step? Steps?

But first I had to think of my children. With their father's exit to heaven, I was forced to deal with their heart-wrenching grief even as I grappled with my own.

Jonathan and Dietlinde arrived a week after we told them the news of their father's death. They would stay for a month. Jonathan had just married Amy Pattison in January. Dietlinde was to graduate that week from Houghton College. She would attend her dad's funeral in Papua New Guinea on the day she should have marched to the tune of "Pomp and Circumstance" with her class.

Just minutes before their flight was to land at Aiyura, the airstrip a couple of miles from our translation support center, another

---

[36] Griffiths, Bill & Cindy. *The Road to Forgiveness.* Nashville:Thomas Nelson, 2001: 120.

flight landed. The flight staff unloaded a coffin. Simultaneously a truck jam-packed with people arrived. Only one Papua New Guinea woman jumped off. Her face and arms covered with ashes, she immediately threw herself across the coffin. The air filled with the bitter wailing and shrieking of this distraught woman. She circled the coffin, banged on it with her fists, all the time pulling her hair. She pounded her chest. At brief intervals she gasped for breath, then the pathetic wailing and groaning continued.

None of the other passengers on the truck came to put an arm around her or stand with her. It seemed she'd gone raving mad from grief. I had no idea who these people were or what personal tragedy this lone woman faced.

My eyes were riveted on the scene when suddenly the announcement of Jonathan and Dietlinde's flight came over the loudspeaker. Heidi, Kurt and I rushed to meet them. As we started to embrace each other, Dietlinde noticed the woman displaying her raw emotions, sprawled over the coffin. It was impossible to ignore her as she wailed, completely absorbed in her own grief story.

"Who is that woman weeping at Daddy's coffin," Dietlinde asked me?

I assured her that this was not her father's casket but a body that had been brought in from some other place. "Now the widow or mother is here with the other relatives," and I pointed to the truck jammed with people, "to gather the body."

We continued our group hug and then I added, "That's why your father and I came to Papua New Guinea, to give the Good News to hopeless people like that."

We sobbed. We huddled. We clung to each other and tried to console each other, determined to value our love for each other more than ever. I had lost a husband, but I hadn't lost everything. I had plenty to live for. I still had four beautiful, precious children. They were particularly precious to me at that moment as we regrouped as a family.

For days I had images of the lonely woman who had gone temporarily "crazy" from grief. In my private moments I wished I could reproduce the wail that engulfed her. The wailing, in some primal way conveyed the anguish I felt. All I could manage were groans that came from deep inside.

Perhaps people in primitive societies have a healthier handle on grief. They seem to be able to cut loose rather than our American way of evasiveness and shallowness.

Still, that scene at the airport was a powerful contrasting image: one woman overcome by her grief, and then our little huddle. Two different nationalities, two different ways of expressing grief, but both caught in the same logjam of emotions that came uninvited with our loss.

But there was another big difference. As shocked and sad as my children and I felt, we could say, "Death isn't a dead end street. We have the assurance that Daddy is safe in heaven. We'll meet him again." In clinging to each other we were also gripping on to God and to the truth we knew.

I wondered if the other woman would ever find hope in her grief journey. Would someone tell her that widows are close to God's heart? What lay ahead for her, for me? Who knew, but the Lord?

Something else was troubling me. One friend, in a pathetic attempt to comfort me, said, "Satan really had the upper hand Thursday afternoon, didn't he?" I was too broken and foggy brained to answer a word. But for days afterward, that thought kept perching in my brain, almost mocking me. *Did Satan really have the upper hand on Thursday afternoon, when Edmund was brutally murdered? Who's really in charge?* Clearly I needed a word from my heavenly Father.

One afternoon I sat in my living room looking through my Bible for something to catch my eye. I wasn't ready to go back to my Read-Through-the-Bible-in-a-Year schedule. I started at the end of the Bible leafing through page after page. I found my answer:

Revelation 22:3 *the throne of God*

Revelation 21:5 *He was seated on the throne*

Revelation 20:2 *Satan is bound*

Revelation 19:4 *they worshipped God who was seated on the throne*

Revelation 18:2 *the home for demons is fallen*

Revelation 17:14 *the Lamb will overcome*

Chapter after chapter describes a God who asserts His kingly control over everything. Heaven rings with songs of worship, one encore after another. Eventually I came to Revelation 1:18 *I hold the keys of death…* He didn't drop the keys on Thursday afternoon, April 29. Satan didn't snatch them from God when He nodded off. God didn't misplace the keys.

Satan doesn't have the upper hand. He never had the upper hand. He never will. God is still firmly on the throne. He doesn't need a seatbelt to keep Himself there. There's one throne in heaven and God is on it. Satan is not on it. No terrorist or earthly king is on it. God is on it. The events of April 29 did not jolt Him from that position. His book tells me I can have confidence in this God, this gracious Father who has a plan.

⧉ CHAPTER TWENTY-TWO

Caught up in praise

It's an awesome God who enables a person to trust Him enough to say against all his natural instincts, 'You know what is best.'[37]

"*T*hen I heard every creature in heaven and on earth and under the earth and on the sea, and all that is in them, singing:

To Him who sits on the throne and to the Lamb be praise and honor and glory and power for ever and ever!"[38]

"I read that verse," said Ross Webb at Edmund's funeral, "to remind us yet again that there IS One who sits on the throne and the events of the past week have not budged Him from that position one little bit."

"Edmund was a man like us," Ross continued. "Frail and dissatisfied with his humanity, as we all are, looking forward, no doubt, to the time he could shake himself free of what he wished he wasn't, and participate in the perfection of Him who sits on the throne.

To Him be praise and honor
and glory and power
for ever and ever!

"We have come to remember Edmund because he was a part of us, made of the same stuff—a husband, a father, a brother, a fellow traveler. Now he is a member of the cloud of witnesses spurring us on to finish our race."

---

[37] Ross Webb speaking at Edmund's funeral
[38] Revelation 5:13

Ross was a co-worker, a fellow-translator. Having just recently completed the translation of Revelation for the Irumu people group of Papua New Guinea, his mind was caught up in the wonder of the majesty of Jesus Christ, so he injected verses about the worship in heaven into the eulogy.

"Beating sun, scorching heat, hunger, thirst, the wearisome burdens, even the real-for-the moment but fast-fading joys of life in a dusty body are but a distant memory for Edmund. It would be nice if he could spare a moment for us who are left. Maybe he is. Then again, joining the angels and archangels and all the company of heaven in singing the Lamb's worth probably saturates a man's being into a single-minded devotion. Will you blame him?"

Ross told the hundreds of people gathered there on May 5, 1993, a little of Edmund's background—his flight from Poland and how, at age sixteen, he yielded his life to the Lord. "Two years later God spoke to him through a missionary slide series." As an aside Ross quipped, "Take courage." A snicker went through the audience. Many of us were missionaries and had intimate knowledge of slides and slide projectors. We wondered if those slide series impacted anyone.

Ross continued, "With a purpose for living he decided to go to seminary rather than carry on the family business. Despite his father's disappointment and refusal to help him financially he did not deny his call and went on to earn his way through by brick laying and tooling. Determination was a hallmark of Edmund's life. Not in vain. It has won him the prize.

Praise and honor and glory and power
to him who sits on the throne
and to the Lamb!

"After three years of seminary, Edmund furthered his education with nurses' training. Then, in 1962 he moved to Canada where he was welcomed, and encouraged in his faith and life goals beyond expectation; and where English became his second language! It wasn't to be his last!

"In Canada, Edmund went to Toronto Bible College and heard about Wycliffe. In 1967 he went to Wycliffe's linguistic training in North Dakota praying all along that God would provide him with a wife who would go to the mission field with him. Little did he know that God would provide him with one who came with experience!"

Ross looked down to where the children and I were sitting. I knew what was coming next. As he told the story I let my mind drift back to my work in Mexico with the Huixtecos. Then to that summer of 1967 when I fell in love with Edmund. I was assigned to be on staff at the North Dakota Summer Institute of Linguistics. I was given the task of interviewing students who were late in arriving, for the candidate office. Yes, Edmund was late... and a fair candidate. He wasted no time in presenting his need to me for a wife. We met every day to pray after that, and were married on August 25th, 1967.

We did jungle camp together (a re-run for me) in November, 1968 and arrived in Papua New Guinea on July the 4th 1969.

Ross continued the story. "On Christmas day, 1969, Edmund and Grace and the recently arrived Jonathan landed at Kasanombe airstrip north of Lae in the rugged Finnistere mountain range of the Huon Peninsula. They settled in Zinsaik village and lived there for the next ten years. During that time Dietlinde, then Heidi and Kurt appeared on the scene and helped (in kids' ways) Edmund and Grace do what translators are supposed to do. God had given them a job to do and they took it very seriously. I venture to say it was to live a life of praise and glory to the ONE who sits on the throne and the Lamb. They did it by committing their lives to translating the words from the LIVING ONE into the Nabak language. Nobody except the author Himself knew that it was written for Edmund to expend his life doing it. What an honor!

"Everyone I have talked to tells me that Edmund was a man of single mind. Recently he wrote, "The difficulties of my childhood years are not something to be mourned over, but served to develop a strong character in me. When I meet hardships in my missionary career, I don't give up quickly."

"Right on, Edmund!

"Life was to prove not so kind at times during the 80's. Edmund's body objected to its limitations. He had scars criss-crossing his body to prove it. His kidneys, back and knees all took their turns at testing his mettle. Grace reckoned that most days of the last twenty years of his life were spent in pain of some kind. He quietly bore the pain and pushed on.

"In February 1980 Edmund, Grace and the children moved down to a large settlement on the outskirts of Lae. Nearly all the men in the Kasanombe area had moved to town. A real wrench to have to leave ten years of friends but there was nothing to do but move to where the action was. The action got hot Christmas that year when they were attacked in their home in the Nabak settlement. Nobody was seriously hurt, Nabak friends surrounded them and they pushed on.

"Only three years later they had to move yet again, this time here to Ukarumpa, our translation support center. It was not their first choice. Most of the friends they have given their lives to don't live here, so Edmund and Grace imported them. Over the last twelve years, many Nabak people have been through Ukarumpa working with Edmund and Grace on translating and checking, including the skillful and dedicated man, Kondo.

Kondo had many friends at Ukarumpa so Ross' next words resonated with them. "Why would God see fit to bring that friendship
and productive period to an abrupt close?" he asked. "He did. Kondo
died suddenly on June 26, 1987 - a week after he was diagnosed as
having liver cancer. Can we understand God?" Ross asked.

And then Ross said something that not only figured into Kondo's
death but would anchor us now during this present tragedy. He
said, "It's an awesome God who enables a person to trust Him
enough to say, against all his natural instincts, 'You know what is
best.' It is an awesome God who works our desperation to His
glory and for our good."

You are worthy, our Lord and God,
to receive glory and honor and power,
for you created all things,
and by your will they were created and have their being.

Ross went on to talk about our frustrations since Kondo's
death and Edmund's single-mindedness to finish the Nabak
New Testament. "Were that I was as driven and single minded.
Will I die at the translation desk, or will God find me at His
appointed time fiddling around?

"I write this down, and I ask Why? for the 100th time. Is
that presumptuous? Fortunately "Why?" is a question that God
patiently listens to. Perhaps He only answers it to the satisfac-
tion of those who get to look him in the face. THEN there is
no question. I guarantee Edmund is asking no questions. He is
caught up in the everlasting praise of the One who with His
blood purchased men for God from every tribe and language
and people and nation. He is on his knees with the Elders before the One whose eyes are like blazing fire and whose feet are
like burnished bronze."

We sang all three verses of Edmund's favorite song, "Through it All".[39] And the choir sang the Negro spiritual "My Soul Is A Witness for My Lord." One line says, "If you get there before I do, tell all my friends I'm coming too." I loved it.

Two men read 1 Corinthians 13 in both English and German. It was awesome to think that those were the words Edmund was contemplating when he was ushered into glory.

My friend Cheryl sang, "May Those Who Come Behind Us Find Us Faithful," which talks about sorting through our things after we're gone. What kind of hints will people find to show we've been faithful to the Lord?

"Tomorrow," I thought, "I will clean out Edmund's closet and desk and let the children decide what they want. Tomorrow we'll talk about when to take the next step." For now, my focus was only on this awesome God who enables me to trust Him and say, "Lord, You know what is best."

---

[39] Crouch, Andrae. "Through it All." Manna Music, Inc., 1999.

Hands through the bars

"There are times when all of us will think that
we've run out of love.
We're convinced that we can't produce love anymore…
Or we wonder if love has died.
No. The good news is that God is love.
The source is as inexhaustible as ever." [40]

I am a Bible translator, but is that all I am? Just someone who exegetes a passage of Scripture and rephrases it in the Nabak language? Is it simply a project? An academic exercise? Is the Bible merely a book, like a dictionary, that I turn to for information?

Or, and this is the crucial question, is this Book the place where I meet with a holy and gracious God who longs to speak to me? Do I translate it only, or do I also have a relationship with the Author that would compel me to obey it?

Since I have organized my life around this Book for many years, what option do I have except to obey, to forgive? Beyond our grief, our Christian faith asked us to remember two things: love and forgiveness.

Unwittingly, I had started the process when I gave the chocolate cake. *Chocolate cake, yes, but could I also extend my hand in forgiveness to his unsteady hand? What would forgiveness look like in this instance?*

---

[40] Shelley, Marshall. "Character Comes Through." *Leadership* Spring 2007: 5.

It was a step I could not do on my own. My children shared my faith in God. Each of them, at a young age, had trusted Christ's love to forgive their sins. Each one showed evidence of desiring to please the Lord Jesus. But they were suffering.

I noted that the passage in Luke 17:1-5, where the disciples asked for increased faith is not in the context of miracles but in the context of forgiveness. We needed a boost to our faith.

Another passage that is often used as a promise of God's presence is Matthew 18:20 *"For where two or three come together in my name, there am I with them."* This verse comes right after the discourse on what to do when a brother sins against you. Following the verse is the parable of the unmerciful servant—the one who had been forgiven a huge debt but wouldn't forgive his fellow servant. This gracious promise of God meeting with us is in the context of forgiveness. It's not talking about coming together for prayer meeting or worship. Isn't God saying that when we've forgiven each other, when we've made things right between us, God will surely show up?

I wanted God to grace us with His presence. Philip Yancey writes, "I never find forgiveness easy, and rarely do I find it completely satisfying. Nagging injustices remain, and the wounds still cause pain. I have to approach God again and again, yielding to him the residue of what I thought I had committed to him long ago. I do so because the Gospels make clear the connection: God forgives my debts as I forgive my debtors."[41]

I would obey, not just in the abstract, but specifically what the Book said about forgiveness. I would give my children good building blocks, just as my father had given me solid building materials for my life. I prayed about my heart attitude and talked to the children. They wanted to do it.

Ten days after "the incident" we drove to Kainantu police station. Behind the station stands a small house with three walls made

---

[41] Yancey, Philip. *What's So Amazing About Grace?* Grand Rapids:Zondervan, 1997: 93.

of brick. The fourth side is only bars, and open to the elements. Kainantu is situated at an altitude of 5,000 feet so even though near the equator, temperatures can drop below 50 degrees. Miliŋnâŋe stood in the corner of the holding cell looking down. A dark gray haze seemed to cover his face. His eyes were bloodshot. Dietlinde cried when she saw him. She had never seen anyone soaked in such despair and looking so ashamed. We all felt sorry for him and one by one reached through the bars to hold his hand. Then we each said the words, "I forgive you," "I forgive you."

Jane Pappenhagen once wrote, "If we love Him, we obey Him. Forgiveness is an agonizing act of obedience, but after the agony we see grace flow, restoring what was broken. God can then continue to use us in His Kingdom work."[42]

I don't have any neat, 7-step formula to tell you how we did it. I only know that when I took the tiny step to give Miliŋnâŋe a piece of cake, the Lord Jesus gave me the strength to take the next step. Perhaps that is what the Psalmist means when he talks about going *"from strength to strength"*.[43]

Though my eyes brimmed with tears, I now caught a clear image of what forgiveness looks like. It is unsteady hands choosing to reach out and grasp another quivering hand. It is grace flowing. Agonizing, outrageous grace. God's grace.

---

[42] Pappenhagen, Jane. "Agonizing Grace." *Intercom* September-December 2005: 16.
[43] Psalm 84:7

Zumbek, our closest Nabak friend with his young family.

Left to Right: Wife Egue, Daughter Nanim, Son Mersi, Zumbek, Eric was not born yet.

Chapter Twenty-Four

Pleasing aroma

"Ready to suffer grief or pain,
Ready to stand the test,...
Ready to go, ready to stay,
Ready my place to fill,
Ready for service, lowly or great,
Ready to do His will...”[44]

Several days passed before I could focus on reading my Bible. I sighed when I saw that my schedule listed Leviticus as the book to be read next. What possible comfort can that be, I thought, but I started in:

"Bring the blood...(1:5)

Skin it, cut it in pieces...(1:6)

Burn all of it on the altar.” (1 9)

Ugh! But then this, *"It is an offering made by fire, an aroma pleasing to the Lord."* As I flipped the pages, those same words were repeated. At each description of a sacrifice, God said it was a "pleasing aroma" to him. At first the words jumped out at me, then they began to soak into my heart like the first refreshing sprinkles of rainy season.

This bloody scene, God said, was a pleasing fragrance to Him? Incredible.

I counted sixteen more times in the book of Leviticus where that phrase, *"an aroma pleasing to the Lord,"* was used to describe a

---

[44] Palmer, S.E.L. and A.C Palmer. "Ready."

sacrifice offered according to God's directions. The scene is not of a nice, orderly butcher shop. No, it talks about chopping up meat, waving it. It describes dipping a finger in the blood and sprinkling it on the priest and on all sides of the altar. Then they were to pour blood at the base of the altar. It must have been a stinky, messy job.

But God looks at it and says, "This pleases me. I like this aroma."

Could it be that the sacrifice of my husband's life was also, in God's eyes, an aroma pleasing to Him?

Fire came out from the presence of the Lord and consumed the offering. Edmund was on the altar. Why should I be surprised when the offering was consumed? What did I think would happen to an offering?

Then I read that the hide, flesh and offal were disposed of outside the camp, burned up. I thought of the bloody rug from the office. Our friends had pulled it up and dragged it to the riverbank. It burned and smoldered for days.

The Apostle Paul talks about a living sacrifice,[45] but in Edmund's case he would be a dying sacrifice. But whether living or dying, what would be the aroma of my life to God?

Lord, may my life or my death be a sweet fragrance to you.

The symbol/motto of the church my sister attends, is a drawing of an ox standing between an altar and a plow. A banner over the scene carries this phrase "READY FOR EITHER." It expresses a sense of dedication to God in the face of two alternatives: service—the plow, or sacrifice—the altar. It begs the question: Am I ready for either?

---

[45] Romans 12:1-2

✌ CHAPTER TWENTY-FIVE

Where were you, lord?

"Faith does not eliminate questions.
But faith knows where to take them."[46]

T he question "Why?" never bothered me as much as the question, "Where were You the afternoon of April 29, Lord?" All through my life I wanted to stay close to the Lord, walking in step with Jesus, never moving away from the place where God could love me. I often recited,

"Keep yourselves in God's love as you wait
for the mercy of our Lord Jesus Christ
to bring you to eternal life."[47]

But that ghastly afternoon of what we call "the incident" I didn't sense God anywhere. I couldn't feel Him. Darkness hovered over the face of the earth.

One night when sleep wouldn't come, all my questions spilled out. "Where were You, Lord? I couldn't see You. Were You even nearby?"

"So, you thought I wasn't there because I didn't stop the axe, is that right?"

"Yes, You're supposed to be All-powerful." *Am I really arguing with God?*

"Are you saying that I could have?"

"Yes, You could have stopped the axe blade in mid-air. After all, You stopped the knife so Abraham didn't kill his son."

"Are you questioning my power?"

---

[46] Elliot, Elisabeth. *A Chance to Die*. New Jersey: Fleming H. Revell, 1987: 55.
[47] Jude 21

"Not exactly. But You could have done something."

"But I didn't, did I?"

"Well, no, obviously You didn't. Instead, You seemed to be hiding."

"Do you know why I didn't?"

"No, I don't know why. How could I?" I blurted out. "I'm not God, after all."

"Do you demand to know why?"

"Welllll, that seems a little blasphemous, doesn't it?"

"Grace, what if I never tell you why?

"That's tough."

"Will you still trust me? Or do you demand to know the secrets of eternity?"

"We're getting in deep, Lord. It's a mouthful but I'll say it, Lord; I'll still trust You whatever. You win."

I was tired; it was too much to think about. I fell back asleep.

A few days later I started the conversation with God again. "Okay, so You have some eternal secret that You don't want to divulge. But I still don't know where You were."

No answer.

I tried reading my Bible. I turned page after page waiting for my tears to stop so I could focus on the words. My eyes landed on Romans 8:34,

"Christ Jesus who died—
more than that, who was raised to life—
is at the right hand of God
and is also interceding for us. "

"Oh, I see it now. That's where You were, You were in heaven praying for me." And I bowed in awe.

Another answer to my burning question came several days later when I read the story of the death of Lazarus. Always before I had come as an outsider to the story in John 11. As an onlooker I had jumped quickly over the sadness and gone right to the resurrection part. But Mary and Martha's story became more understandable to me after Edmund's death. I could now stand inside their experience. And there it was. Two simple words: *"Jesus wept."* No longer a Bible trivia question—What's the shortest verse in the Bible? Those two words became the most important words in the Bible for me.

"That's where You were, Lord. You were weeping with me." Praying for me. Weeping with me. Asking me to trust You.

Symbol for the American Association of Baptist Churches:
Ready for Either.

◈ CHAPTER TWENTY-SIX

The dwarf

*"Real Christians know that
Dark Thoughts can rain on
their parade.
But they have the umbrella
of choice
to shelter them as they march."* [48]

I stand by the river that flows at the back of our house at the translation support center. The river, at flood stage, rushes with maddening force down to the gorge. Suddenly a cyclone whips through our yard twisting a huge mango tree until it breaks and slams into the river, roots and all.

The swift current carries it downstream. To my dismay many of my personal items hang in the branches of that tree. I catch a glimpse of my favorite books, my clothes, a file drawer and some treasured knickknacks. I stand frozen on the bank staring at this uprooted tree.

Then, as if someone has given me a shove, I fly along the bank desperately trying to catch up with the tree as it dashes about in the wild flow of the river. No matter how hard I run, it is out of reach. Soon I am out of breath, and can only watch as it races around a bend and out of sight.

---

[48] Landorf, Joyce. *Monday Through Saturday.* Waco: Word, 1984: 34.

In despair I fall to the ground hopelessly staring in the direction where the grand tree has vanished. I cry for this beloved tree that has stood tall and borne luscious fruit. Previously, I had often sat in its shade. My children enjoyed climbing the tree. An inner tube hung from one of the lower branches giving hours of fun to children in the neighborhood. Friends remarked on how sturdy the tree appeared even though it was not native to this country. Now it was gone.

Out of this frenzied gloom, a fat little dwarf approaches. His white beard glistens in the sun. He is richly dressed in a shirt designed for an elf, leather jerkin and green knickers. A wide black belt held it all together. He focuses his keen eyes on me. "It's gone, Grace, and it's not coming back," he says in a most gentle tone. "But we have work to do here."

For the first time I notice his large hands. These are hardworking hands. He bends over and picks up bricks from a stack nearby. With amazing dexterity and swiftness, he slaps mortar on each brick. No weak and doddering old man he. Within seconds, a sturdy wall takes shape as this strong and robust man works.

I no longer feel engaged with the disappearance of the tree, but decide to work shoulder to shoulder with this likable, though mysterious, little man. We don't talk any more, but I feel strangely comfortable with him. He takes charge and I just follow his lead, placing one brick on top of another, until the wall stands about three feet high.

Then I wake up. *"I'm not standing by the river; there's no brick wall."* Squeezing my eyes tightly I want to hang on to the dream, to stay in this other world. Slowly I surrender to the reality that this is Thursday, two weeks after my husband's death. I open my eyes slowly, still savoring the sweet presence of the dwarf.

The dream's meaning is obvious. Without a doubt the mighty tree represents my husband, and part of me has gone with him. Immediately I perceive that the little man is the Holy Spirit.

How reassuring, I think, that he didn't say, "There is work to do," and step aside leaving me to it. Instead, he lingered and demonstrated how to handle the bricks. His bearing, his dignified companionship quieted me. I wasn't alone after all.

In those waking moments a song floated from the recesses of my memory into my senses. I recognized it as a tune that our twins had often sung as part of a highschool singing ministry. *There is a Redeemer* was a piece of music in the repertoire of songs they performed in four-part harmony—

"There is a Redeemer, Jesus, God's own Son/
Precious Lamb of God, Messiah, Holy One/
Thank You, O my Father, for giving us Your Son/
And leaving Your Spirit 'til the work on earth is done." [49]

The thought that God's Spirit was present to provide whatever I needed soothed me. In the chaos of this frightful and dark situation in which I now found myself, the truth that He was active and available had slipped my mind.

In my many years of living with the Nabak people, I loved watching babies sleep in a net bag hanging down their mother's back. These traditional, hand-woven bags provide the mother's warmth while keeping the mother's hands free. She can reach her hand behind her and give a little pat if the baby stirs. Completely oblivious to any danger, the baby is contented just to sense their mother's nearness. In a similar way, at that moment, I felt the Holy Spirit's warm and loving presence.

The dream would not change my loss or my grief. Nothing could reverse my husband's tragic death, but the dream helped

---

[49] Green, Melody. "There is a Redeemer." Birdwing Music/Cherry Lane Music Pub. Co., Inc., 1982.

me understand I had choices to make. I could either be paralyzed and sit forever staring down the river, or I could stand up and do something constructive. Was God calling me to continue the task of Bible translation for which Edmund had expended his life? If so, it felt much less forbidding and remote now.

The dream and its powerful message not only challenged me to get on living, but also put my heart at rest. Somewhere through the murk, a thread of hope began to weave itself in and out of this wreckage. I was held in His net bag, close and secure.

CHAPTER TWENTY-SEVEN

What do I do now?

"It is obvious to me that each new day—along with all the persons and events of that day—does in fact question us, if we will submit to the test. The death of a dear one asks me what I really believe about death and how profitably I can confront loss and loneliness... Suffering asks me if I really believe I can grow through adversity."[50]

"**G**o!"

"No, stay!"

"We serve notice to vacate this house."

"Finish the job."

"They'll kill you."

"I'm sure you can do it."

"Just shake off the dust and go home."

Nothing could undo the dreadful thing that had happened. It was like some stray dog had grabbed the fabric of our lives and shaken it viciously between its teeth.

That moment of Edmund's murder divided our lives between a "before" and an "after". We weren't a perfect family in the past but our family was intact. Now we felt torn and dragged through the mud. And that's when the voices started.

First, there were the voices of my co-workers. They hugged me and said how shocked and sorry they were for my loss. I loved them for helping me keep my head above water.

---

[50] Powell, John. *Fully Human Fully Alive*. Niles, Illinois: Argus Communications, 1976: 92.

But certain local men added their hostile and belligerent voices saying the property where my house and several others at our translation support base was located, belonged to them. It was a lie, of course. The day after Jonathan and his wife Amy and my daughter Dietlinde returned to the U.S.A. after the funeral, rocks were thrown on the roof of my house.

Fires were deliberately set, burning down trees my husband had planted. One night they burned down the beautiful picnic table our son had designed and built in our back yard. They stole my strawberries and chopped down my banana trees and hibiscus hedge. I had to hire someone to guard the backyard so clothes wouldn't be stolen from the line. One morning I found a message on my front porch, "Go home, Piss off."

Widows in this country, I was told, are considered the weak members of a tribal society and should be ostracized. These attackers were not Nabak people, but people from a language group living a short distance from our center of operations. I felt very vulnerable. One Sunday while we attended church, a group of vandals broke the windows and screens of our living room and carried off two of our mattresses and several blankets.

Once, when we walked outside, a man stood across the road and pointed his machete at us. The message was unmistakable. The panic attacks I suffered through my childhood threatened to return. These men scared me.

One day a young man knocked at our door. He said he was taking a survey. "How many rooms in your house? Is there a bathroom? What appliances do you have?" he asked.

"Why are you asking these questions?" I queried.

He told me that the leaders from his village were hiring a lawyer to assess the value of the property and claim that I was an illegal resident.

I asked, "How old are you?"

"I think I'm 17," he replied. "Why?"

"Do you realize, young man, that I have lived in this house before you were ever born. It's curious that you think the house belongs to you when you weren't even born yet. You only need to look at the legal documents and you will see that the property belongs to our Institute."

He continued to ply me with questions. "How many cats do you have? Do you own a dog?"

"You must be kidding," I said. "You think that my cat is also yours?" I laughed and closed the door. But I was not laughing inside. I turned to the office and made back-ups of all our files, packed our valuables and photos and took them to a safe place.

We were not squatting illegally; the government had leased it to us for linguistic research. Some of my co-workers also lived on the section of property that the locals called 'disputed land.' They, along with myself, were directed to attend an emergency meeting. Our administrator said that the choice was ours—to move to the Guest House, or to stay in our homes. The decision was unanimous. We would stay in our homes.

My sister Kathryn and a friend had traveled around the world to visit us. I had to tell them of the uneasy situation they had walked into. Kathryn said, "If you stay, we're going to stay with you." It was a tense atmosphere, not the pleasant relaxing visit I wanted, but they saw firsthand the battle we faced. Two more voices were added to the chaos. That year I received eleven eviction notices.

Still another voice came from a personnel consultant in my organization. He wrote, "I encourage you to continue with the New Testament on your own. Others have done it and I'm sure you can too." Living thousands of miles away in a safe suburb of

America, I'm sure that his words sounded reasonable, like what a dedicated missionary should do. I took his letter, threw it on the floor and stamped on it.

"You have no idea what you're suggesting," I spoke to no one in particular. Don't get me wrong. I love Bible translation. I just didn't like the wrapping it came in for me personally. I hadn't signed up for murder. I hadn't signed up for fires, rock attacks and eviction notices.

I started to write an answer to his letter, "Have you ever awakened in the morning with the realization that someone wants to kill you? It messes up your whole day..." I wrote for five more pages but never mailed the letter. It was therapeutic to spill my frustration onto paper.

The fearful suggestions of friends back in America joined in the maddening jumble of voices. One supporter wrote, "The Bible tells us that when people don't accept us we should wipe the dust off our feet and get out of there." She noted the Bible reference of Matthew 9:14. I pondered and prayed over the passage. I'm not sure I ever reconciled "shaking off the dust" with the following verses about being sent out as "sheep among wolves." That voice banged around in my head for days.

Others wondered why we wouldn't leave the country, at least for a break, but I couldn't. There would be a murder trial and since I was the first witness on the scene, I was required to appear in court.

All these different messages churned and screamed in my head, begging to be listened to, begging for an answer. Obviously, I needed to hear from my Lord. My scheduled Bible reading for June 12 took me to 2 Kings 6. There I found the words of Elisha's servant echoing in my own head, "What shall we do?"

Hadn't I fairly screamed those exact words in prayer many times in the last few days? I, like that servant, was also feeling the danger all around me. Wasn't it enough that my heart was grieving, that our feelings of loss for our husband and father went deep?

Then came Elisha's faith-filled words spoken with authority and clarity, "Don't be afraid. Those who are with us are more than those who are with them." God opened the servant's eyes, "And he saw the hills full of horses and chariots of fire all around." [51]

My journal for that day simply says, "Elisha's story is God's word for me today." In the margin of my Bible I wrote, "Wow! My army, God's protecting power is bigger and more powerful than theirs."

From then on whenever fear came sneaking up to grab me in its vice, I cried, "Open my eyes, Lord. Let me see your horses and chariots of fire."

No, it wasn't a magical solution to my dilemma. The dangers were still very real. The threats didn't stop. In fact, even a year later when I came back from furlough, rocks were thrown through my window. The verbal threats continued. A mob of people blockaded the area. I made the choice to not live in fear. In pure, gut-level faith I went outside and served the hoodlums cold drinks, coffee and cookies. God's voice had won over all the other voices.

One Friday evening three hooded vandals broke in. I was standing by my dining room table. I screamed. Usually when I'm scared my muscles tighten up and I can't squeak out a word, but that night I screamed. I grabbed a chair and pointed the four legs at them like a lion tamer. One man slashed out with his machete crashing it into the chair. He left a huge gash in the chair but missed my fingers by an inch.

I didn't see any angels or horses of fire but the three vandals backed out the door. The next day I kept my schedule of traveling

[51] 2 Kings 6:16-17

with one of my co-workers up to Mt. Hagen in the Western Highlands Province, to teach a Translation Principles course for two weeks at the major Bible College in Papua New Guinea. From screaming, I lost my voice, but got it back in time to start teaching on Monday morning.

I determined, with angels and horses of fire on my side, that my choices would grow out of a place of power, not fear and insecurity. Two powerful truths would be my guiding lights: the power of the presence of a sovereign, omnipotent God, the power of the promises in His inerrant Word.

CHAPTER TWENTY-EIGHT

Keep following

*"In simple trust like theirs who heard,
beside the Syrian sea,
the gracious calling of the Lord,
let us, like them, without a word,.
Rise up and follow Thee."[52]*

Many times in the days that followed Edmund's death, I cried
as I read my Bible. It seemed that every verse I read carried a
special message for me. I filled several journals. Something began happening deep inside of me as I soaked up God's Word. I
fell in love with 2 Corinthians. I read the first few verses and
thought, "These are key verses on suffering."

I had graduated from Bible College where we studied Doc-
trine 101, then Systematic Theology. I had written a long and
detailed doctrinal statement when I joined Wycliffe. I could
explain inerrancy of Scripture and discuss intelligently the
doctrines of Christ and the Holy Spirit. I was well trained
in the application of justification and the essential nature
of man. I could discuss the trinity or the return of Christ.
What I lacked was a theology of suffering. It doesn't matter
how well you're trained; there are some things you only learn
through experience.

---

[52] Whittier, John Greenleaf. "Dear God and Father of Mankind."

I had read Foxe's Book of Martyrs as a teen-ager, but at the time it seemed ancient. I knew for sure that if that kind of persecution came my way I wouldn't fearlessly go on a death march. And I certainly wouldn't be singing. *People like that belong to a different strata of society, don't they?*

But now I faced a hostile situation. God had not kept me from losing my "Benjamin,"[53] but I read 2 Corinthians 2:14-15, "*Thanks be to God, who always leads us in triumphal procession in Christ and through us spreads everywhere the fragrance of the knowledge of him. For we are to God the aroma of Christ...*" And I wrote in my journal, "Oh, for the perfume of Christ within me to be in evidence to all around me."

I saw things in God's Word which I hadn't seen before. I read in 2 Corinthians 5:2, "Meanwhile we groan."

I agreed wholeheartedly.

Then God whispered, "But it says 'meanwhile.' It's not a forever thing."

This new, intimate relationship with Jesus where He shared sweet thoughts from His Word with me renewed my strength, restored my perspective.

One day as I read John 21 I realized it was a replay of a scene a few chapters earlier. In the first scene, in John 18, Peter sits around the fire in the morning, and disowns his Lord. Not once, not twice but three times. Shameful.

In the second scene, after the resurrection, the disciples and Jesus are at the shore, again, early in the morning, and a fire of burning coals is there. Jesus speaks first to the group (John 21:5-14) but then He zeroes in on the person who has a problem, Peter (15-22). This passage stands between the old Peter and the new Peter. Three times he answers the question that Jesus asks and the

---

[53] Genesis 42:33-44:34

relationship between Peter and Jesus is rebuilt. There's that amazing grace of Jesus that forgives Peter. Then, in great tenderness, Jesus recommissions him with the words, *"Feed my sheep"* (vs. 17). Restoration and fellowship and service. Isn't that outrageous? I thought of Miliŋnâŋe. His name means "mercy on us." Don't we all need God's mercy resting on us?

Then this curious passage follows, *"When you were younger you dressed yourself and went where you wanted; but when you are old you will stretch out your hands, and someone else will dress you and lead you where you do not want to go."* As I read those words I said, "I'm on a path I don't want to go either."

The next verse says, *"Jesus said this to indicate **the kind of death by which Peter would glorify God.**"* I was startled by those words, "the kind of death." Thoughts came uninvited. Could Edmund's death also glorify God? Could the "kind of death" he suffered, the ugliness of his murder glorify God? Honestly, I had never thought about death being a way to bring glory to God, and certainly not a particular kind of death bringing glory to God.

It wasn't just Peter's death that would bring glory to God. Jesus said, "the kind of death." Tradition tells us that Peter was crucified upside down.

It sent me on a search through the Word. I wanted to learn how we bring glory to God. I discovered that it isn't only in our worship and in miracles that God is glorified. Confessing sin also brought glory to God (Joshua 7:19). And when the whole earth hears of His glorious name, it is filled with his glory (Psalm 72:19). Then I was back in 2 Corinthians. In 3:18 Paul talks about us reflecting God's glory as we are transformed into His image. "Lord, I want to be a mirror that reflects your glory" I whispered. "If in some mysterious way you receive glory through the kind of death Edmund went through, then I surrender him to you and to your plan."

I read on in John 21 to Peter's question about what would happen to the other disciple. Jesus' answer is straightforward, "It's really not your concern what happens to him. You must follow me." Those were my directions. I heard no other specific or detailed outline for my future, just this. *That's it? Keep following?*

I craved a promise, some reassurance of safety, but this was all. God wasn't showing me the script for the new role He wanted me to play in His grand drama. Just "Follow Me." And His words sounded more like a gentle invitation than an assignment.

I would wait on God, keep walking, following Him. I would lay down the grief because Kondo had died. Let the past be past. I would not focus on the "Why?" of Edmund's death. My job? Keep following.

By God's grace that's what I'll do.

In time, I knew, He would chart the details of the new course for me to follow.

✂ CHAPTER TWENTY-NINE

A one-talent man

"In almost anything I offer to Christ, my reaction would be,
'what is the good of that?'
The use He makes of it is none of my business;
it is His business, it is His blessing.
Whatever it is,
which at the moment is God's means of testing my faith
and bringing me to the recognition of who He is—
that is the thing I can offer." [54]

I walked to church by myself. Usually Edmund and I would walk together, but he was walking the streets of gold. The twins had already left earlier for Sunday School. I asked the Lord to walk with me and keep me company.

In church I felt more comfortable sitting toward the back. I felt like I was detached from reality. I didn't understand how life could go on as usual when my world had turned upside down.

Church is a good place to cry. I couldn't pinpoint exactly why I was crying. Was it that I missed Edmund? Was I mourning things I had said, or had not said? Maybe I was revisiting sad places from my past? Maybe I cried because of the burden that God had laid on me for Miliŋnâŋe? Maybe it was a little of everything. I teared up as we sang,

---

[54] Elliot, Elizabeth. *Worldwide Challenge*. January 1978: 39-40.

"God of the ages, History's Maker,
Planning our pathway, Holding us fast,
Shaping in mercy All that concerns us:
Father, we praise You, Lord of the past.

God of this morning, Gladly Your children
Worship before You, Trustingly bow:
Teach us to know You Always among us,
Quietly sov'reign—Lord of our now."

The fact that we had put years of energy into the Nabak program and now it was at a stand still, seemed to fade as we sang the next verse:

"God of tomorrow, Strong Overcomer,
Princes of darkness Own Your command:
What then can harm us? We are Your people,
Now and forever Kept by Your hand."[55]

The spiritual welfare committee at our translation and linguistic center organizes the topics and speakers for each Sunday's meeting. Today Carl Campbell spoke on the parable of the talents from Matthew 25:14. The story is of a master who is ready to embark on a journey. First, he entrusts various amounts of money to his servants. One receives five "talents", an amount of money well over $100,000. Another receives less than half of that, two "talents". The third servant receives only one "talent", about $10,000.

The differing amounts are based on their differing abilities. "Not everyone is given the same responsibility," Carl said. He

[55] Clarkson, Margaret. "God of the Ages." Hope Publishing, 1983.

talked about God tapping us on the shoulder and how we need to be willing to use our gifts and skills for His glory.

All the time, I'm looking ahead in the story and feeling sorry for the one-talent man. *He got short changed, then on top of that, the master speaks such harsh words to him. Why? He was afraid. So? Well, I'm afraid. What's wrong with that?*

Then Carl said, "Each of us can be productive. It's our responsibility to advance the kingdom of God through the wise use of our gifts. Even if we have only one talent, we can't sit on it."

He went on to tell how the two servants invested their giftedness and so earned Jesus' commendation, "Good and faithful servant."

"The problem with the one-talent man," Carl said, "is not that he received less than the others. He's not scolded for being afraid. The harsh words are spoken because he didn't even try. It is never a wise move to bury our gifts, our responsibilities."

That Sunday I went home and knelt beside my bed. "Okay Lord, I hear you. I feel you tapping me on the shoulder. I'll try my hand at the translation. I only promise to try. I know it will be an unmitigated disaster, but I'll try. If the translation turns out to be a flop, I'll blame you. You got me into this."

A few days later a woman came to the door. "I have a message from the men of my village. They are giving you two days to move out of your house."

By this time I was absolutely convinced that God wanted me to finish the translation project so I said, "God hasn't told me to leave."

"Well, these 'big men' are giving you two days," she repeated.

Refusing to let darkness and fear hover over my heart, I said, "I'm doing a great work here of translating God's Holy Book for the people who speak Nabak. So you tell those men that I'm not leaving."

She started wringing her hands. "Oh, but you must leave. I'm really scared for you. They will come and kill you."

"Well," I said, "if they come, I'm just one woman. I'm not strong enough to fight against them. They can kill me, but if they do, I'm very scared what will happen to them. God has told me to stay. If they kill me because I stay, then they will have to explain to Almighty God what they did."

She was very quiet as I served her tea and biscuits and sent her on her way. I don't know if she passed on my message, but I continued to live in my home, ignored the voices and din around me and moved ahead on the translation.

◈ CHAPTER THIRTY

A pair of shoes

"What this dying world could use is a willing man of God
Who dares to go against the grain and work without applause...
Whose love is tough and gentle a man whose word is sure.
God doesn't need an orator who knows just what to say...
He doesn't need an army to guarantee a win
He just needs a few good men." [56]

At Jonathan and Amy's home church, Union Bible Church, they held a memorial service for Edmund. It was one of our supporting churches, one that we attended while on furlough. We had many dear friends there.

After a beautiful eulogy Pastor Waugh held up a pair of shoes. "Who is going to step into Edmund's shoes now that he has gone to glory?" And he set the shoes on the platform.

Jonathan told me later, "Mom, I got up from my pew and walked up to the front. I stepped to the platform and put my feet into those shoes. I believe God is calling me to come back to Papua New Guinea and help you finish the Nabak New Testament for which Daddy gave his life."

The violent and unexpected death of his father led our son Jonathan to re-examine his own life and his goal of becoming a millionaire by age 25. He and his wife Amy and baby Isaac arrived

---

[56] Gaither Vocal Band

in Papua New Guinea on August 6, 1994 to help me finish the Nabak translation project. For Jonathan, it was coming home. For Amy, it would be a whole new life. She hadn't dreamed of such a thing when she married him, just four months before the murder. But she loved him and now went with him. *Thank you, Jesus, for this beautiful, dedicated young couple.*

Almost immediately, Jonathan started helping me and the Nabak translation team dub the words of the newly translated Gospel of Luke onto the movie of the Life of Christ, commonly known as the Jesus film. It would be the first movie in the Nabak language.

We crowded into a small room where Lauren Runia, the technician, had fastened egg cartons on the walls to make it soundproof for recording. The biggest challenge was to fit the long, complicated Nabak sentences into the short space allotted for each scene. He displayed incredible patience as we repeated one section over and over again until the words fit perfectly.

The Nabak people weren't that practiced in reading their language fluently, and to add to their stress, we shoved microphones in front of them. But in short order they caught on, and soon became whizzes at reading and dramatizing. Sisi read the words of Jesus; Zeŋge, Kondo's wife, said the parts of the women in the script. Zumbek was chosen to be the narrator. Jonathan said Zacchaeus' lines and we all laughed. It was so good to see smiles again.

Because the Nabak people are very interested in how things came to be, we decided to add a section from Genesis at the beginning of the Luke script. Zumbek, as narrator, bridged the gap in time between the Creation scenes and the first chapter of Luke. He said, "That part is the story of God creating everything, and then what went wrong in His beautiful world. Now in the following scenes you will see what God did to remedy the problem." Everyone on the team liked the effect of the Genesis prelude.

Weeks later the film was ready for showing. We said good-bye to Jonathan and Zumbek. The two of them traveled first to Nabak settlements around the coastal town of Lae—Bumayong, Situm, Kamseleŋ, Tepmamen, Second Seven. At least 1,200 people came to the showing at Poom.

After leaving the coastal towns they traveled to Zinsaik, the first place we lived when we arrived in the country in 1969. Back in those days our four-month old Jonathan had no trouble winning the hearts of the Nabak people.

Now he was back as an adult. Astonished, the old ladies came to check him out. They only had to look into his eyes to know that, "Yes, that's Jonathan alright!"

With a perfect view of Papua New Guinea's third highest mountain, Mt. Bangeta, it was the perfect setting for the showing of the Jesus film. At least 1,000 people came to see it.

The next day, after tearful good-byes, Zumbek, Jonathan and a string of young people hiked on to other mountain villages: Sasawalen and Kalaŋan, then to Baindoang, Kiakum, Sakalang, Kwabeling, Yalumban, Tukwambet... Slippery logs span the swift-flowing rivers in Nabak territory. They crossed the same river several times in one day. The trees and jungle thickened but they kept plowing ahead, one behind the other. As they climbed higher, there were fewer mosquitoes, but then there were leeches. They were exhausted and ready to stop, but the local Nabak men leading the way kept putting one bare foot ahead of the other. There are no road maps or signposts but they never got lost. After six weeks of hiking, they eventually reached all fifty-three of the Nabak villages.

Everywhere, the Nabak people were surprised to see Jonathan and Zumbek, but especially Jonathan. They gave them their best food—steaming bowls of wild sugar cane shoots dipped in spicy pandanus sauce, field corn, pumpkin leaves and, of course, heaping plates of sweet potatoes.

The Nabak have little material wealth, but they do have the gift of hospitality. They treated the two men royally. The doors to their houses are so low Jonathan had to duck as he entered, but he loved it. Sleeping on split-bamboo floors and showering in cold, mountain streams were no hardship.s

The two read the Nabak Scriptures with the villagers and played ball with them. Everywhere smiling faces and warm handshakes greeted them. When darkness fell they started the film. Since the movie is five hours long, bedtime was always late.

The village leader was often the one who would host Jonathan and Zumbek. At one village, after a long hike and the late night movie, Jonathan and Zumbek returned to the leader's house to sleep for the night. Their host Mineyu said, "I've rolled out your bed mats," then pointed to a heap of firewood in the corner. "The fire is blazing and there's enough wood so you can stay warm all night. As for myself, I won't be sleeping, but everything is ready for you to sleep."

They wondered why he wouldn't be sleeping, but they stretched out on the floor and slept themselves.

The next morning Mineyu gathered the people of the village together. First, he arranged the carriers to tote the movie equipment to the next village. The elders gave speeches, the only right thing to do when important visitors come. They also gave gifts of appreciation to Jonathan and Zumbek.

Then the old leader said, "My friends, I must tell you what is burning in my insides. Last night I could not sleep. Instead I sat up all night gazing into the fire. Sitting hunched over like that, near the fire, I was deep in thought through the night. He explained, "Two unusual events came to my attention yesterday and I needed to consider the meaning of them."

"The first thing is that last night, in the movie, we saw how they crucified Jesus. I didn't know it was like that. I think it's incredible, you know, the suffering, the mean way they treated Him. I couldn't get those scenes from the movie out of my mind. We've heard the gospel; the early missionaries and evangelists told us about Jesus. But, I tell you frankly, I never saw Him like I did last night. Hearing it in my own language helped me understand it. I needed some time and quiet to ponder that."

Mineyu stepped back then looked at the ground. "The second thing is that Jonathan has come back to us. That, too, is unexpected." His eyes roamed over the crowd. "You know what it's like in this country. We always seek revenge. Getting even with those who have harmed us is what we do best. Our ancestors practiced pay back and we gladly carry on the tradition.

"But Jonathan, he's back to help us even after we killed his father."

"I had to sit beside the fire and think about these two extraordinary events. You agree, don't you, that nothing like this has ever happened here?"

"*Penaŋ. Kogok.*" "True. It's like that," they answered. Each one was thinking of revenge killings in their own family.

Mineyu continued. "Like banana leaves sway and bend in the breeze, my thoughts and questions turned and twisted in my mind all through the night. I kept asking myself, 'What is the deep meaning to these happenings? What is the message for the Nabak people in these two strange events?' These are not common, everyday circumstances. What's going on here? It was a riddle I had to solve."

The mothers quieted their children. The men leaned forward. "With the first soft light of dawn, my insides were also illuminated," he said. "I understand it quite plainly now."

Even the village dogs quit their yapping. It seemed everyone and everything paused and waited for the riddle's solution. "Listen. Are you listening?" he said. "I now know what the message is for us Nabak people."

In hushed whispers the crowd indicated that they were ready for the answer to the questions that had perplexed Mineyu all night. So he continued, "Here is the wisdom we must take from these two events. I'm telling you now that the forgiveness that Jonathan and his family have demonstrated by coming back to us, is the same kind of forgiveness that Jesus showed when he died on the cross to forgive us our sins."

He swung his arm to make the shape of a cross. "I have found the deep meaning I was searching for," he said.

Everyone nodded soberly. Something important had just transpired. They could feel it. In fact, it marked the turning point for the Nabak people in understanding why in the world these crazy "white skins" had come to live among them.

Hearing these words, Jonathan struggled to choke back the tears. *Here I am, just me, one young man standing miles from nowhere. I'm out here on an island in the middle of the Pacific but You are using me. I wondered what I could possibly do by coming back to the Nabak people. Now, Lord, look what You've done. I, too, see it quite plainly. God, You are so Almighty You can use even me.*

Jonathan was crying so hard he could not say a word at first when they held the bullhorn for him to speak. The tears would emphasize his message. He finally spoke, but not words he had rehearsed or scripted. God gave him the words. Later he couldn't recall the words. He only knew they came from some place deep within him and that the whole village was crying.

As Jonathan and Zumbek reported the story to me, I imagined God saying, *"Grace, I was there all the time with you and Edmund—in the sewing classes, the writers' workshops, the medical work, youth camps, the translation. I was always at work among the Nabak people. But, you see, they needed an object lesson. Now they have it."*

Jonathan Fabian hiking with baby Isaac.

⚝ CHAPTER THIRTY-ONE

Drop by drop

"He who learns must suffer.
And even in our sleep
Pain that cannot forget
Falls drop by drop upon the heart,
And in our own despair,
Against our will,
Comes wisdom to us
By the awful Grace of God." [57]

Zumbek, who had been struggling with Edmund's death in his own way, came back to work with us. "Even with this tragedy, we must finish the translation for my people," he said. We tried, but it was extremely painful to see Edmund's handwritten notes. We couldn't bear to be in his office. We couldn't concentrate. Our emotions were spent. One inner voice said, "You can do this." But at the same time I had no strength or energy. Sometimes we would sit at the translation desk only crying and praying, crying and praying some more.

One morning a new idea floated into my brain. "You know, Zumbek, these epistles are too difficult for us to wrestle with right now. Why don't we go back and read through some of the <u>easier narrative</u> passages?"

[57] Aeschylus.

"Let's go to the Gospel of Mark," he suggested.

"Yes, that was the first book we translated. We know it's pretty good."

And so we agreed. We printed two fresh copies from the computer and settled into a new routine. Occasionally Zumbek would suggest a slightly different wording of a verse. My quick eye found a couple of spelling mistakes but mostly we let the flow of Nabak words carry us along.

The parable of the sower was a strong reminder that the good seed, the Word of God, planted in hearts, would produce a crop.

As we read of Jesus stilling the storm, the havoc of our pain-saturated circumstances seemed less severe. "He's in our boat too," I said. "It doesn't minimize the danger, but He's with us."

"I'm glad He is," Zumbek added.

And why did we smile when we came to the story of John the Baptist beheaded? We both remembered that the translation consultant who was checking our translation against the Greek had asked, "Why did Herodias' wife want the head put on a platter?"

The old Nabak man checking translation with us had laughed when I joked, "Maybe it was so she could eat it?"

Cannibalism had been outlawed in Papua New Guinea, but it was still in the memories of some. The Nabak group was far removed from that, but just so there would be no confusion we added some implied information, "So she would know for sure that John the Baptizer was dead."

The hours slipped by easily. After coffee break we read about Jesus' transfiguration in chapter 9. In that story, Peter, enthralled that Moses and Elijah had showed up, suggested building three huts, one for each. But the voice from heaven said, "No, Peter. You have it wrong. It's not about Moses; it's not about Elijah.

My beloved Son, Jesus is the focus here. Listen to Him." Zumbek and I stopped to pray and to listen, hoping that we might hear that voice.

"I'm sure God is telling us to continue with this translation in spite of the tragedy, in spite of the harassment," Zumbek said. "Things haven't turned out the way we wanted, but I know deep down inside that going ahead with the translation is the right trail to take."

I showed Zumbek the chart of translation progress, the same one I had showed my family at breakfast on that fateful Thursday. "See, we're at 77%." We studied it for a few minutes. Hesitantly, but sure of God's embrace of encouragement, we continued.

That afternoon we came to Mark 14 and the story of the woman who poured expensive perfume over Jesus' head. In Nabak they like to say things in parallel, first the negative, then the same thought in a positive sentence. So verse three says, "She did not parcel it out drop by drop, she poured it on Jesus' head." As I read the passage, those words gripped me. Here was a woman who showed her great devotion to the Lord.

Immediately the despicable scene in Edmund's office flashed to my mind. The gory, horrible picture of my husband after being murdered, the axe, his blood pouring down—it all came back in one terrifying, big-screen drama. And then the awful drip, drip, drip of his blood in the clinic. I knew in that moment that Edmund's blood was my very expensive perfume. Tears came in buckets. Zumbek was not sure what had triggered my grief.

Finally I was able to tell him. "It's those words 'drop by drop'. I think the Lord is saying, 'Grace, will you totally relinquish Edmund, or will you reluctantly, drop by drop, give him to Me?' "

Like the woman anointing Jesus, I also, out of my highest esteem for Jesus, released Edmund. "You are worthy of my best."

The next verses say that others were quick to judge and said, "Why this waste?"

But Jesus' response was, "She has done a beautiful work of showing her sacrificial love for me." And with those words I sensed that Jesus was also affirming me and letting me know that it is not a waste to give our most precious treasure, something considered extremely costly, to Him. He is simply worthy.

After that deeply moving experience, when flashbacks of the gory scene started to replay in my mind, a more peaceful image replaced it. I could see Jesus in the office and I put myself there with him. I was now the woman pouring out my own expensive perfume to Jesus. The translation office was transformed to a place of worship.

Where was Jesus? I had the answer. I now knew exactly where He had been that Thursday afternoon. He was right there with me, accepting my precious love offering.

☒ CHAPTER THIRTY-TWO

Amazing grace

*"'Twas grace that taught my heart to fear,
And grace my fears relieved;
How precious did that grace appear
The hour I first believed."* [58]

Every month since my husband's death Zumbek and I traveled to the jail to visit Miliŋnâŋe. Fifteen months later, May, 1994, when the court psychiatrist transferred Miliŋnâŋe to the psychiatric ward at the hospital, under guard, he was given medication and his hallucinations subsided. He stopped pacing. He could reason logically, like he had years before as a trained and wise headmaster of the elementary school. Now we could talk, though he never broached the subject of "the incident."

In the trade language of Papua New Guinea we describe a skinny person as "bone nothing." Miliŋnâŋe fit that description exactly, so I always took a picnic lunch for us. The guard allowed us to sit together on the grass in the backyard of the hospital grounds, to eat and visit with him.

We also packed some newly translated Nabak Scripture portions and asked Miliŋnâŋe to check them for any mistakes in grammar, or confusing phrases. On each visit we'd hand him new work and collect the chapters we had left the previous time.

---

[58] Newton, John. "Amazing Grace." 1779.

But this afternoon in 1994, after Miliŋnâŋe handed us the passages of Scripture he had checked, he asked, "Would you like to see the hymns I wrote?" Of course we said we would love to.

"I go to all the church meetings here at the hospital," he explained. "I'm learning different tunes. Then I come back to my room and write Nabak words to fit." We stayed and sang all twenty-three of Miliŋnâŋe's hymns.

One tune he was singing I immediately recognized as the old and familiar hymn, "Amazing Grace." Miliŋnâŋe's lyrics read, *"Because of your Son my sins are forgiven."* Zumbek and I looked over his shoulder to the words penned in his notebook. We joined in on the next line. *"Because of your blood my sins are forgiven."* Miliŋnâŋe's voice sputtered and cracked on the next line, *"Because of your grace..."* He broke down and sobbed.

The tears welled up in my eyes and wet my cheeks. Zumbek could not hold back his tears. Even the prison guard, a non-Nabak, choked up. He did not understand the Nabak words but he recognized that something very profound happened right there.

As we sat in the hospital yard that day, I knew that indeed God's grace is amazing. Precious. Outrageous. His kindness to my family and me was remarkable. That His loving-kindness extended to the Nabak people, including my brother, Miliŋnâŋe, was also marvelous.

The three of us joined hands and sang the rest of the hymn together. But in truth, we were not just three. There were four of us, for God's presence flowed around us and over us.

"We are standing on holy ground,

And I know that there are angels all around.

Let us praise Jesus now.

We are standing in His presence on holy ground."[59]

---

[59] Davis, Geron

⚅ CHAPTER THIRTY-THREE

Day in court

> *"Everyone asks me about the court decision*
> *and about the man who killed you.*
> *They hope that there will be a big settlement.*
> *They want to see him punished.*
> *And what if he is? What if he is tortured?*
> *What if his loss makes me rich?*
> *Neither money nor revenge*
> *will bring you back.*
> *There is no victory for me in a court."*[60]

More than a year after "the incident," a man known as Brother Andrew came to the house to talk to me about Miliŋnâŋe. Dr. Brother Andrew is a retired Anglican priest. He said he would be the court psychiatrist. He turned out to be not only the psychiatrist but also the investigator.

He asked me questions about Miliŋnâŋe's role in Edmund's death. Then he talked with Dr. Helen, the one who had attended Edmund at the clinic. He was the one who transferred Miliŋnâŋe to the psychiatric ward of Goroka Hospital, the same hospital where I had received six pints of blood at Dietlinde's birth; the same hospital where Kurt and Heidi were born.

After being postponed five different times, Miliŋnâŋe's hearing was finally scheduled for November 24, 1995, twenty months after

---

[60] D'Arcy, Paula. *Song for Sarah*. Wheaton: Harold Shaw, 1979: 63.

the crime. All four children went along with Zumbek and me. I, as the first witness on the scene, did not know if they would call me to testify. That was the only reason I dreaded this event—having to regurgitate the bloody details of that awful afternoon.

We all knew what the outcome of the court case would be. Murder is a federal crime in Papua New Guinea. Miliŋnâŋe had confessed to the murder. There was no evidence to the contrary. Reports surfaced that explained how an upstanding school principal could become a murderer. Stories indicated that he displayed psychotic behavior and had become disconnected from reality.

He was already in jail. In my mind there was really no need to even have this court case, except to satisfy the requirements of the justice system. He would stay in jail. Case closed.

Never having been involved in the court system in my own country or in Papua New Guinea, I didn't know quite what to expect. I noticed when we had lunch at the nearby hotel that I didn't have a pen with me. Ever the person to take notes on sermons, write in my journal and make endless TO DO lists, I stepped into the little stationery store and bought a notebook and pen.

We sat in the gallery. The only other people in the courtroom were Miliŋnâŋe's wife and daughter. The daughter had become deathly ill with malaria while doing her student teaching and had been sent to this hospital. Her mother Mutalac had come to be with her and at the same time see what was happening to Miliŋnâŋe.

The state prosecutor Christine Ashton, from Great Britain, came and shook hands with me, thanking me for being forgiving and gracious to Miliŋnâŋe, then went and sat near Dr. Andrew in the front. Miliŋnâŋe was brought in, unfettered, but sitting beside a prison guard. I could not determine the role of everyone sitting up front, but expected I would learn.

The judge, wearing a white curly wig and black robe, came in from the back. We stood. The state prosecutor started the proceedings, "On April 29, 1993," and she paused, waiting for the court secretary. I realized then that the secretary did not have a computer or typewriter, but was writing every word in longhand. I reached into my purse and pulled out my new notebook and pen and started writing. The session was excruciatingly slow because of the need to capture everything on paper. The satisfying part was that I could write down every word.

Miliŋnâŋe comes from a prestigious line, with a nephew who was governor, another relative in leadership with the Lutheran Synod and a cousin who was a judge. But it still surprised me that someone in Miliŋnâŋe's family had hired a lawyer for him.

This lawyer stood up and gave a report that was full of lies and half-truths. He painted a picture of a man who served as a community school teacher. The lawyer never said that Miliŋnâŋe was retrenched from that job, and also from being coordinator of the College of Distant Studies, because of his psychotic behavior. The lawyer said he was employed as a Bible translator since he left the Department of Education in 1986. The truth was he had only worked with us away from his home for six weeks in 1988 then again in March of 1993 one day short of six weeks.

I had not hired a lawyer because I assumed that the state prosecutor would make sure the truth was told. She used the police reports and psychiatrist's report and did not challenge Miliŋnâŋe's lawyer.

I was sure the court psychiatrist, when giving his report, would talk about Miliŋnâŋe's schizophrenic episodes. Instead he referred to the auditory hallucinations and abnormal thought patterns as "atypical psychosis, diagnostic manual 298.90."

Now the court was not only excruciatingly slow, it was emotionally agonizing. "A little truth here would help," I wrote in my notebook.

Beforehand I had dreaded the idea of standing up in court and giving testimony. Now I wished for a chance to shout out the truth.

After the hearing we were told there would to be two weeks until the sentencing. During that time, Zumbek and I double checked our information, and wrote up a three-page report giving evidence contrary to the reports presented in court. I believe the Bible teaches that if we don't voice the truth about criminal activity then we are participating in it.[61] I could not remain passive and live with my conscience.

At the hearing the report was that Miliŋnâŋe manifested auditory hallucinations only when away from his family for long periods of time. Also they stated that he was under duress because we were forcing him to finish the translation. They implied that he had a stellar résumé.

Our report told that the elders in the village said he once chased people with a knife, and how he also often left his house early in the morning and did not return until after dark. They said sometimes Miliŋnâŋe went into hiding for several days. I wrote down names and eyewitness accounts. "People are afraid for their children because he lives next to the village school," the elders said.

I went carefully through my own transcript of the hearing and lined up the discrepancies. I closed my report by saying, "A great tragedy has already occurred. If you send Miliŋnâŋe back to the village, without medicine, can you guarantee that the compulsive, psychotic thoughts won't come again? If he would kill his wife or some other person in the village, that would be a travesty. I don't want anyone else to go through the same heartache our family has experienced these two years."

---

[61] Leviticus 5:1

I sent my report to the judge, the state prosecutor and to the court psychiatrist. After receiving my letter, Dr. Andrew flew out to Miliŋnâŋe's village. True to their culture, the same people who had told us the disturbing news of Miliŋnâŋe's condition would not say these same facts to Dr. Andrew.

Brooks Peterson in his book *Cultural Intelligence*, says it well, "By failing to say 'No' when that is what they meant, they were not lying; rather they may have felt it was best to be indirect in order to keep things harmonious...Many people around the world often choose to take the approach of 'telling the Americans what they want to hear' because they may feel that to be truly direct could lead to useless or counter-productive conflict."[62]

Having studied the Nabak culture and lived among them for many years, I knew that in their sociocultural system they did not see their two versions as a contradiction. It would bring too much shame to admit these things to an outsider. They needed to cover up the weakness and maintain good relationships in the community.

I went directly to the state prosecutor and she told me, without flinching, that she would not appeal. She did not state any reason for holding that position. My letter was generally disregarded. On December 2, 1995, at the sentencing the judge ruled that Miliŋnâŋe's sentence be four years in jail. Miliŋnâŋe had already served 20 months. The judge suspended the remaining part of the sentence and said he should return to his village. "You are free but on a three-year bond of good behavior."

No one was appointed his caretaker. No provision was made for his medication. Since he lived far from any health facility, all the good help he had received was discontinued. He was abandoned to a distraught family and to a community, that,

---

[62] Peterson, Brooks. *Cultural Intelligence*. Yarmouth, Maine: Intercultural Press, 2004: 39.

though beautiful in many ways, was ill-equipped to manage this potentially dangerous situation.

I don't know what else I could have done to get the truth out there. I never wanted harsh treatment for Miliŋnâŋe. If they had meted out a severe sentence I would have been the first to argue for grace. Why couldn't he at least receive the medicine he needed?

I also felt he and his clan should be given some responsibility for Miliŋnâŋe's actions. I had often witnessed how the Nabaks worked out restitution when someone had committed a crime. There would be bags of yams to replace the stolen ones, or a pig given to repay damage done. Was it too much to ask that they provide someone to take Miliŋnâŋe's place in the translation project?

Right after the sentencing, while Miliŋnâŋe stayed in the courtroom to finalize his release papers, Zumbek and I, along with Miliŋnâŋe's wife, went out to the courtyard. Zumbek said to Mutalac, "Well, he's released now and will go back to the village, so I guess you'll have to be in charge of him."

She said, "Oh, don't say that. I don't want to be responsible for that man." And then she went on to tell of all the abuse and threats she had received from him previous to his killing Edmund. We stood only five or six feet from the door of the courtroom where the lawyer had just talked about his wonderful family and community where he would be secure, and it would be wrong to keep him in jail.

I thought how easy it is for people, in the safety of their halls of justice, to make this kind of decision. I'm sure no one in the courtroom that day would be willing to take a person with atypical psychosis into his home if he were not on medicine. Were they oblivious to the fact that they were handing a poor, uneducated village woman a huge and risky responsibility?

With tears in my eyes I shook hands with Miliŋnâŋe. I worried about him without medication. I asked, "Is it alright to still send translation to you to be checked, if I can find a way to mail it to you?" I had enjoyed working with Miliŋnâŋe while he was in the psychiatric ward. Perhaps seeing him calm and cared for gave some meaning to Edmund's death. I felt that he was a prize we had gained through this very costly sacrifice of Edmund's life.

Miliŋnâŋe said, "No, you better not. People might think it is the studying and reading that I do that makes me crazy. They might blame you."

I hugged Mutalac. We cried. I could read the apprehension in her eyes. She had been so brave through the months of bearing the stigma of her husband's crime. But now she must cope with an erratic man.

Rather than closure after the court case, I was haunted by questions. Should I have hired a lawyer? But I don't have that kind of money. Should I appeal? Would the outcome be any different if I did? How would the Nabak people perceive it if I did? This was something I would have to work through a few times, toss it around, lay it out, sweep it up.

I ran to God's Word and finally peace began to flow into all the nooks and crannies. My guiding light came from First Peter 2:21-23 "*Christ also suffered for you, leaving you an example for you to follow in His steps,*

—who committed no sin,

—nor was any deceit found in his mouth

—and while being reviled, He did not revile in return,

—while suffering he uttered no threats,

—but kept entrusting Himself to Him who judges righteously."

By God's grace I would release the whole thing into His hands. That was the only safe place. I could not threaten, or grumble or disparage. The whole tangled mess of knots should rest in His capable, wise hands. If anybody could untangle the knots, He could.

There would be no winners in this courtroom, but as a child of God I could be a victor. Simply by putting my faith in this One who judges righteously, I was a winner.

❦ CHAPTER THIRTY-FOUR

Roots and all

"Break thou the bread of life, dear Lord, to me,
As thou didst break the loaves beside the sea;
Throughout the sacred page I seek thee, Lord,
My spirit pants for thee, O Living Word."[63]

I made this journal entry a few days after the courtroom experience:

"I'm reading Acts 27, about Paul being in a terrible storm while on board ship. That would have been bad enough but he was a prisoner. I'm sure he did some mighty heavy praying, but the storm got worse. When he tried to give advice it went unheeded. He even got to the edge of hope and thought maybe it was the end.

"But then an angel came in the night. He told Paul not to be afraid. Easy for the angel to say, he wasn't on the ship. But the real punch line is that God is going to spare them all because He wants Paul to stand trial. A strange deliverance, wouldn't you say?

"I am reminded by this story that:

—Angels visit in the night,

—God's ways and purposes are not like ours,

—He often uses storms,

—He rarely delivers us so we can lie on the beach and get a tan after the storm passes,

---

[63] Lathbury, Mary A., "Break Thou the Bread of Life." 1877.

—Most of the time no one will understand God's ways and many will think it's hopeless,

—When the angel visits take fresh courage."

Well, I saw no angel but a turning point occurred a few days later as I reflected on the courtroom drama. Fulfilling Edmund's legacy, I would return to the translation desk. I was changed by the events of the last two years. With my Bible open I felt a new energy, and embraced this opportunity to finish the Nabak translation. I believe it was the Holy Spirit providing the wind beneath my wings. I felt His gentle touch on my shoulder saying, "Don't give up. Just wait and see what I can do."

But now the Book of Romans stared at me. I was scared of that daunting task before us. I even scolded Edmund for leaving me before finishing that part of the New Testament.

Zumbek, and I took fresh courage and started in. I had expected it to be much more difficult than it really was. We found Paul's debate very logical except the rhetorical questions. For instance, in Romans 8:31-39 Paul is not asking questions for information. "Who shall separate us from the love of Christ?" Paul and the people in the Greco-Roman world of his day would know that the answer is, "No one."

The Nabaks do not have this grammatical device in their language. They immediately start asking, "Who can separate us? Let me think now." So we changed the question to a statement, "No one can separate us from the love of Christ. Absolutely nothing can separate us from the love of Christ." Then the list of specific situations follows and each one is eliminated as a threat to our security. The rephrasing resulted in correct and satisfying comprehension. We liked the flow of the Nabak words.

Every day during the translation process I thanked the Lord for bringing Zumbek to help me. *"There's no way I could do this on my own,"* I thought.

Zumbek had graduated near the top of his class from a three-year Bible College, then studied another five years at Seminary. He was well qualified for this job. When we leaned back and relaxed after finishing all sixteen chapters, I said, "Well, Zumbek, I know you studied the Book of Romans in Bible College, and then again in Seminary, so you already know Romans pretty well. Was it helpful to go through it again," I asked?

"Yes, it's true I studied the Book of Romans. I knew what it said. In a manner of speaking, I understood its leaves and branches. But now I comprehend its *yaŋaŋ*, if you know what I mean," he said.

When the Nabak people describe a tree they use this word *yaŋaŋ* to describe the lowest part of the trunk and the whole root system. Zumbek was telling me that when he studied the book of Romans in English he had understood the surface things, but when he heard it in his own mother tongue he grasped its deep meaning.

This was a satisfying result for our hard work and a good place to pause. I would be leaving for a year's furlough in June, so we decided as a family in February, 1995 to hike through Nabak land.

On this trip we would trek along just one of the three major mountain ranges where the Nabak people live. To start, we flew in a Cessna 206 to the short slanting airstrip where Edmund, newborn Jonathan and I started out in the Nabak program on Christmas Day, 1969.

I had forgotten how beautiful the mountains were. I marveled that the pilot could find his way through the maze of jungle-covered mountains.

How many times in years past had we waited at this Kasanombe airstrip for a precious mailbag, school supplies or fresh meat. In some ways it seemed that nothing had changed. Dark-skinned children still frolicked ahead of us on the trail. Swaying bridges still crossed the gorges, and petite women still carried heavy loads in net bags—babies, garden produce, firewood.

It has to be one of the most gorgeous places in the world. In fact, the mountains are so beautiful it hurts. The air is pure and the nighttime sky breathtaking.

But we had changed. Instead of our four young children, four grownups stepped out of the plane. Jonathan came back with his wife Amy to help me finish the translation project. They carried my first precious grandson, Isaac. Dietlinde had come back to teach missionaries' children. Our twins were born on Papua New Guinea's independence day. Someone in the hospital had suggested I name them "Inde" and "Pendence." But I didn't. Now Heidi and Kurt would graduate from high school in June and return to the U.S. for college. I could hardly believe that God had graced me with these incredible children.

The biggest change though, was that instead of Edmund, we brought printed copies of his challenging biography written in Nabak by Zumbek. The people wept unashamedly with us when they saw us and glimpsed Edmund's picture on the cover of the book.

I prepared for weeks for this hike but it was a tough climb along the ridges. It took hours to scramble down, only to hike up the other side. In some places the trail was so steep my foot kicked dust or stones into the face of the person behind me. A poem by Amy Carmichael says it beautifully:

"Long is the way, and very steep the slope,
Strengthen me once again, O God of Hope.

Far, very far, the summit doth appear;
But Thou art near my God, but Thou art near.
And Thou wilt give me with my daily food,
Powers of endurance, courage, fortitude..." [64]

As we hiked from village to village people could not be hospitable enough. They gave us their best in every way. Greens of all varieties: pumpkin leaves, cucumber leaves, castor oil leaves kept all their vitamins when steamed in bamboo. Field corn grilled over the coals and sweet potatoes roasted in the coals were standard fare. The savory, sweet taste of homegrown coffee stayed on my tongue for hours. My favorite of all was chicken cooked in coconut milk. We were more than just white people passing through. Our suffering, theirs and ours, created a bond of kinship. Giving food was one little way they could make restitution and assuage the guilt they felt.

We thought, as we hiked from one place to another, that our loads would get lighter because of selling Nabak books. But in each place they loaded us with gifts of handmade net bags, potatoes, cucumbers and oranges. We ended up with more weight than we had taken.

In one village a teenage girl gave me a net bag with eggs and cucumbers. Her mother said, "You delivered her and her twin sister years ago when I had complications." I remembered the situation exactly.

Deep joy replaced aching muscles as people welcomed us warmly. One dear friend, Fuave, even came in the middle of the night to stir up our fire.

People eagerly bought Scripture books, readers and Edmund's story. A leader in Sasawalen, a tiny village carved out of the side

---

[64] Carmichael, Amy. *Toward Jerusalem.* Fort Washington: Christian Literature Crusade, 1961: 52.

of a mountain, said, "We never dreamed you'd ever come and visit our little place." All along the way little Isaac added many Nabaks to his list of admirers.

In the evenings Jonathan and Zumbek set up the projector and showed the life of Christ movie taken from the Gospel of Luke. Deep joy changed to awe as we heard people wail while watching the scenes of the crucifixion of Christ.

One night as we got ready for bed, all feeling exhausted, Amy said, "Everybody say what you are thankful for."

Jonathan said, "Just being here."

Amy said, "I'm thankful that I have a nice toilet at home. I really don't care for outhouses or trying to hit the hole."

Heidi said, "The beautiful scenery."

Kurt said, "I'm happy to be here and to know that Daddy had already tramped these same trails."

Dietlinde said she liked the change of pace from teaching school every day.

I said, "I'm thankful for the strength to be here and meet old friends."

The last day was the toughest hike of all. First, we hiked through the rain forest for a good two hours, all down hill. At the bottom, when our knees were shaking, we had to cross a bamboo bridge that crossed a swift river charging through a narrow gorge.

Then a landslide closed the trail. The only way around was up. I was grateful for a helping hand over the rocks and boulders for the next phase of the trip. It was not as steep as some places but for hours we just climbed and climbed, steadily upwards.

Then as we climbed down the other side we found we could breathe easier at the lower altitude but we sweated from the increased heat. Not many trees shaded us. The hottest and most uncomfortable time was tramping through wild sugar cane. The trail, if you could call it that, was just wide enough for one person. The wild sugar cane scratched and cut our arms.

Seven long hours later, at 3:00 p.m. we arrived at our transportation spot. We traveled the rest of the way by Land Rover.

Our carriers? They turned around and walked back home. They figured they could make it in three hours. They had carried the generator, gas tank, Isaac's crib, all the Nabak books, our sleeping bags and clothes. We only carried ourselves. What amazing people, never complaining about our slow pace or heavy loads.

Thank you, Lord. It's a privilege to have a wee part in what you're doing here. I knew that there was still a steep climb ahead of us to actually finish the translation. Just before Edmund's death we published a newsletter with a ladder going up the side. On each rung we printed the name of one book of the Bible. Then near the top I drew an elf to show how far we had come in the translation task. I said to Edmund, "I really need to put two elves up there, one for you and one for me."

He said, "That would make it too crowded. It's only a drawing. Leave it with one." Little did we dream that just days after we mailed out that newsletter, I would be left to scale the rest of the ladder by myself. "Strengthen me once again, O God of Hope, Far, very far, the summit doth appear."

God of grace, Deepen my trust. Sustain me as I climb.

Grace and Zumbek in their most typical work position: surrounded by commentaries, rough drafts of the translated text in hand, computer on, various translations of the Bible nearby for reference.

✂ CHAPTER THIRTY-FIVE

One old man

"There is a 'grace awakening' loose in the land. Will you become a part of it?" [65]

The extroverted Nabak people love to sing and dance. Dramas come naturally. They planned an over-the-top ceremony for the dedication of the Nabak New Testament for August of 1998—not just one celebration but two.

The first one took place on the outskirts of the large coastal town of Lae from August 13-16. They wanted the first day just for our family. My sister and her husband, Mary and Ed, flew from the U.S. to join us for the celebration. The women joined arms with Mary, Heidi and me to dance. The men showed Ed and Jonathan and Kurt how to dance and play the drums. We feasted and talked the day away.

The next day several thousand more Nabak people arrived and a hundred or more visitors. The air was heavy with the scent of frangipani, and ruby-red hibiscus bushes lined the road. Women plucked the blossoms and stuck them in their hair. We felt the tropical heat and swatted at mosquitoes.

Nabak dancers in full costume met us at the road. They wore headdresses made from the beautiful feathers of the bird of paradise (the national emblem) and the black quills of the cassowary.

[65] Swindoll, Charles R. *The Grace Awakening.* Nashville: W Publishing Group, 1996: 308.

I knew that the dancers would have risen early to preen and prepare for their part by putting on face paint, loops of beads, and large, beautifully patterned shells. Some wore nose ornaments of pig tusks. Many had tucked ferns or palm leaves into their intricately woven armbands.

Following behind the dancers and the call of drums, we were escorted to the large sports field. My family rode on the back of a red truck. Cartons of Nabak New Testaments were piled on the truck. They were wrapped like a package in a red cloth, then tied with red rope. This was highly symbolic for the Nabak people, for everyone knew the story of the red knot.

A Nabak man dressed in a traditional loincloth stood in the truck with us. He swung a bullroarer around and around as we drove in. The loud whirr like the sound of wind drew everyone's attention and reminded me of the wind of the Holy Spirit blowing over us and around us.

This beginning to the celebration was a particularly powerful moment for us and for the thousands of Nabaks lining the perimeter of the sports field.

The clause "tying the knot" is the expression the Nabak people use to translate the word covenant or agreement. The title on the cover of the Nabak New Testament is appropriate—*Kawawaŋgalen Tâtâ Alakŋaŋ*, GOD'S NEW KNOT.

On one side of the field stood a temporary structure for the sound system and where announcements were given. Nearby was the table where New Testaments would be sold. On the far end they had built a covered area where the visitors could sit out of the sun.

After singing and dancing, Sisi walked to the center of the sports oval. Everyone laughed because of his odd costume, a necktie and a loin cloth. He came crying and blowing his nose into a long handkerchief that he carried in his net bag. He paced back and forth. "Life is so sad," he said between wailing and pulling out more lengths of the handkerchief.

Though 3,000 or more people stood encircling the field he had everyone's attention. "My friend has died, I feel sick and old. Nothing goes right. Oh, life is no good." Sob, sob, sob. "I'm unhappy." With the stating of each sad event he pulled out more and more of the long handkerchief and snorted into it.

He continued his lament and then seeing a little chair nearby sat down. The chair collapsed. "Why I can't even sit down," and the sobs and moans continued.

Then I approached Sisi and touched him gently on the shoulder, *"Notn, kulekiyet omba tasunik?"* My friend, why are you crying so hard?" I asked. "Look, I brought a present for you."

He brightened. "Maybe my troubles are over." But then he looked at the label hanging from the beautifully wrapped package. "But this says, 'This is a gift for everyone.'" He broke into loud weeping again. "It says that it's a gift for everyone but there's only one gift. Look at all these thousands of people! How could one gift be for everyone?"

Then Zumbek joined us and spoke, "My brother, why don't you open the package and let's see what it is?"

Sisi turned to the crowd. "This man is really smart. Did you hear what he said? He said to open the present. That's a good idea isn't it?"

My children came up then and all of us helped unwrap this package. It was a Nabak New Testament. Sisi lifted the beautiful book high in the air. Its gilded edges reflected the sunlight, and the crowd erupted with clapping and shouting, crying. It was the most beautiful sound I have ever heard.

Sisi turned around so everyone could catch their first glimpse of the book. He looked up at it the whole time. Then he noticed the red ribbon bookmarkers. "Do those ribbons have any meaning?"

"Yes," I said, "they have deep meaning. The ribbon stands for the covenant that God has made with us. He has tied His knot with us. The red stands for the blood of Christ shed on the cross."

Sisi lowered the Bible and opened it at the place marked by the red ribbon. In loud, clear voice he read the words, *"Kawawaŋaŋaŋ ningat tikŋaŋ penaŋ namndeye keyepmti egaŋ nin keŋ taolet omba minndamti Zisas Kilais ek ndamukulem mti yomengatnan ndatitiyet zempeme msalen kapi kwatoge. Wa ken in nnaŋgat pembenaŋgapmti yek."* *"For it is by grace you have been saved, through faith—and this not from yourselves, it is the gift of God…"* [66]

"Ah, now I understand why it's a gift for everyone," Sisi said. "God's grace is for everyone and it is this book that tells us about this wonderful gift." [67] He closed the book and held it close to his chest with both arms.

Completely unexpectedly someone stepped out of the crowd. It was Manepe. "Let me see that book," he said. After looking it over he asked, "I wonder if this is the book the old man is always talking about. You know who I mean. Where is that old man who is always talking about the book?" He let his eyes wander over the crowd.

Finally Papa Siŋgema stepped out from the crowd. Dear Papa, the one who had prayed down Father, Son and Holy Spirit while we checked the Gospel of John. The one who had charged us with finishing the translation. He was still alive, having out-

---

[66] Ephesians 2:8-9

[67] Ed Swanson wrote the original script "The Treasure" for his puppet ministry. The Nabak people and I adapted and expanded that script as a drama to be performed at the dedication ceremonies of the Nabak New Testament.

lived the two men he had charged to finish the translation. Papa hobbled forward on his cane, his back bent over almost double. He wore thick glasses.

"Oh, there you are," Manepe said. "Here, Papa. They have this book. Would this happen to be the book you've been talking about for years?"

Papa took the book and held it just inches from his face. He turned it over, rubbed its cover. Then with tears streaming down his face he said, "Oh, yes, this is the book I've been waiting for. This is it." Clasping it lovingly close to his chest he said, "Now I can die. I've seen the book."

When the first proof copy of the New Testament had arrived at our house months earlier I had turned every page. There was a message from God for me on each page. "Grace, I kept my promise. I didn't leave you. I gave you strength. I carried you. I love you. I didn't forget you, I wiped your tears, I held you and guided you. I took care of you. I heard your prayers…"

And now I heard the heart and words of Papa. I could not restrain the tears as I saw those New Testaments come out from under that red cloth and into the hands of the Nabak people. Could our reward be any sweeter than this?

Grace Fabian and Zumbek Molong overcome with joy at the first Nabak New Testament Dedication, August 14, 1998. The rain didn't keep the three thousand Nabaks away.

❧ Chapter Thirty-Six

A good science lesson

"The greatest sermon I ever heard
Was sung to me by a wounded bird" [68]

Every day of the celebrations for the completion of the Nabak New Testament there were more dramas, special singing and speeches. Someone had written a special liturgy for the occasion. It was very meaningful. In one drama they reenacted the coming of the first evangelists. Another showed their first taste of salt, and seeing matches for the first time. They are an oral culture and these stories are passed from one generation to the next.

Every clan had their own repertoire of song and dances. They all wanted to add their talent. They often think in pictures and one skit showed this aspect of their culture perfectly

Once a year the Nabak people celebrate the yam festival. The word for year and the word for yam is the same, because it takes one year from planting time for the yam to be harvested. At a yam festival time they plant a long pole in the ground. They tie the largest yams on the pole. All the other yams are piled around the base of the pole. The prize-winning yam, the longest and fattest one, is tied to the very top of the pole.

After feasting and singing and dancing the yams are distributed to every family in the community. It is a kind of welfare

[68] Bauer, Fred. *For Rainy Mondays and Other Dry Spells.* New York: Prometheus, 1973: 81.

system to make sure that every family will have food for the coming year.

To prepare for one skit at the dedication ceremonies, men gathered Bibles from nearby language groups, a Bible in the trade language and another in a coastal language. They climbed the yam pole and tied these at different heights on the yam pole. They had planted this pole, the height of a flag pole, in the middle of the soccer field. They climbed to the very top of the pole and tied a Nabak New Testament. "This one wins the prize. This is the best yam of all," they said. In all my years of living among the Nabak people, I had never seen anything like that joyous celebration.

Later in the day James Mineyu came over to the table to pick up his New Testament. He had the card with him to show he had pre-bought one. We handed his new New Testament to him. James looked it over and seemed to be studying it. I wondered if maybe there was a flaw in his copy. I was about to go to him and ask, "Is there something wrong with the book?" when he walked out to the center of the sports oval.

He stood erect, waving his brown-covered Nabak New Testament high in the air. "This reminds me of a *kambun*," he shouted to the crowd of around three thousand Nabak people at the New Testament dedication ceremonies.

What was James talking about? Let me explain. A certain butterfly living in the Papua New Guinea rainforest lays hundreds of eggs. When hatched, the larvae crawl up a particular tree and munch on the leaves. When their grub-like bodies are fat and almost ready to burst, they crawl part way down the tree trunk and start constructing a protective tent. They make this using the silk from their own bodies.

When the soft, oval-shaped covering is finished, all but three larvae crawl behind it. Those three stay on the outside, fold in the edges of the *kambun,* and then fasten it to the bark of the tree by secreting a resinous substance from their bodies. They seal it all around, making it perfectly secure for the other larvae inside. When their work is finished, they drop off the outside of the *kambun,* fall to the ground, and die.

Securely concealed inside this big silk nest, the rest of the larvae are safe to grow and eventually pupate. Just as they are about to metamorphose, they gnaw a little hole in the *kambun* and emerge from their safe tent. Like a golden sunrise, suddenly dazzling yellow butterflies fill the sky and fly away up the river together.

The Nabaks know the habits of these delicate creatures, but James went on, "Think about it," he said, gripping his brand new New Testament, "We need to live inside the *kambun* of God's Word. Now we have it in our own language, so we can crawl inside it. If we stay in God's Word like the larvae stay inside their *kambun,* our *insides* (hearts) will grow strong."

James looked around at the crowd while lovingly caressing his New Testament. Another concept was forming in his mind, "And while we grow, we'll be protected from sin and temptation just like the little insects are shielded from the rain and cold."

He paused and took a deep breath, giving time for his analogy to settle into the minds of the audience: "Just as the larvae live together as a colony inside their *kambun,* we Nabak people can live as a strong, harmonious community and church when we're inside God's Word."

He waited to let that settle into his listener's minds. Then he continued in his expressive voice, "My fellow Nabaks, we have the chance to live in this *kambun* and be changed. Inside our new *kambun* we can be born again. God wants to make us into something beautiful."

Then, he looked around, and shuffled his feet. He spoke slowly with a tinge of emotion in his voice, "And don't forget that some people have given their lives so we can live inside this Word of God. Our fellow Nabak, Kondo, worked faithfully to translate the Bible for us." James sighed. "Then he died with his beloved translation on the pillow beside him." They remembered.

"Then the white man, the second-born son, Amuŋ, Edmund, was killed by one of us." Quiet fell over the group. Heads went down as James continued his analogy.

"The third we all know was Jesus. Most importantly, Jesus died so we could have life. Those three died so that we could be safe in our own *kambun*."

All this deeply moved the Nabaks as James' words sank in. I sat mesmerized by this object lesson. I pressed my Nabak New Testament to me. *Thank you Lord for your outrageous grace to us.* I felt light of heart because of a Nabak man who was so spiritually responsive.

Afterwards I went to James and told him how his analogy had touched me deeply.

"You liked that?"

"Yes, very much."

"Wait here," he said as he dashed off to his house. He returned with a *kambun*, a gift to me.

As I touched the softness of the chestnut brown *kambun*, I marveled at its construction. Dots of the sticky substance still remained along the edges. I couldn't help but wonder how those little larvae chose the three who would stay on the outside and die. Who knew that Kondo would die on June 26,

1987? That Edmund would die on April 29, 1993? That God's own Son would die?

"For truly in this city there were gathered together against Your holy servant Jesus, whom You anointed, both Herod and Pontius Pilate, with the Gentiles and the peoples of Israel, to do whatever Your hand and Your plan had predestined to take place." [69]

Thank you, Lord, that in your own beautiful and mysterious way You are using all things—three little larvae, the deaths of Kondo, Edmund and, yes, Jesus, to fulfill Your purposes.

As I pondered James' words my mind whizzed back over the years. I must admit that sometimes I asked, "Am I doing the right thing? Will it make any difference? Isn't it crazy to stay here this long?" But now, hearing James' analogy, my heart overflowed with gratitude for my years with the Nabak people and all they have taught me. I'm truly thankful for God's Word always guiding, comforting and strengthening me. I know that living inside God's *kambun,* my heart can be at rest.

The festivities for the first celebration culminated with Miliŋnâŋe's brother, Moses, on behalf of the Sanau clan, giving each one of my children, grandchildren and myself gifts of their traditional wealth. My gift was a peace headband. "Tying the head" is the Nabak expression for reconciliation. I was being introduced to another powerful ceremony involving knots. As Moses tied it on my forehead, he said, "I have started the ritual here and they will finish it up at the mountain village of Baindoang."

That was the only hint I had that I would soon be witnessing the most remarkable and touching ritual of my many years among the Nabak people.

---

[69] Acts 4:27

Papa Siŋgema (in white) is the old man who thought he would die before the completion of the New Testament translation, but at the dedication he was the first to receive a copy. "Now I can die because I have seen the book and held it in my hands."

✂ CHAPTER THIRTY-SEVEN

Triumphal procession

"At the cross, at the cross where I first saw the light,
And the burden of my heart rolled away
It was there by faith I received my sight
And now I am happy all the day." [70]

On August 18, two days after the first dedication celebrations we flew to Baindoang, Miliŋnâŋe's village, for the second dedication service up in the mountains. Miliŋnâŋe would not be there. Mutalac had sent word to me that Miliŋnâŋe had committed suicide. The trail between the airstrip and the village of Baindoang had been cleared, and it was thrilling to be part of the beautiful procession of men carrying the cartons of Nabak New Testaments up the mountainside. At various spots along the trail women gathered to sing a welcome song, and to offer us much needed refreshment of fresh fruit—passion fruit, oranges and bananas. They had soaked the fruit in the river to keep it cold.

As we arrived at the edge of the village a group of women greeted us. They sang another welcoming song and told us to follow the flower-strewn pathway leading around the outskirts of the village.

The flower petals and leaves on the path led us to a village "gate" beautifully decorated with flowers and a banner with the words, "Following in the Footsteps of Jesus." The local pastor

---

[70] Watts, Isaac.

on the inside of the gate led in prayer and Zumbek, the co-translator of the New Testament, responded from our side of the gate with a prayer.

This custom is carried over from their days of tribal fighting, when they needed evidence that the visitor was a friend or foe. A friend would give a greeting. A foe would not answer. Now as Christians, someone inside would pray. Then the visitor would also pray. That would be the sign of friendship between those arriving and the residents.

I was given the honor of cutting the "ribbon" that would open the gate. Two rows of people dressed in traditional loin cloths and string skirts lined the pathway on the other side of the gate, but before walking forward, the leader of the ceremonies said that we would now set apart several minutes of quiet to remember and honor those who had worked on the translation, but who were now dead. Four people were specified: Sanaŋkepe Buni, a Nabak school teacher who had helped us in the beginning stages of language learning, Kondo Siŋema who worked with us for twelve years, Miliŋnâŋe Sanau and Edmund Fabian.

As the names were spoken, the people on the other side of the gate fell to their knees and bowed their heads. Everything was perfectly quiet except for the gentle sobbing of people. They had not attended Edmund's funeral, but now they were showing their deep respect for him.

My tears flowedfreely. It was wonderfully healing to join with my friends in our sorrow. Oh, how my family and I had grieved over our loss, but the Nabak people had suffered deeply too. The love coming from these people to me was so real I could almost touch it. Those moments are indelibly engraved on my heart.

After this time of reflection and weeping together, the people lining the pathway stood up, and I realized that all of them were members of the Sanau clan. Miliŋnâŋe's widow was the first to greet me. We hugged each other for a few moments, and she and her clan members put garlands of flowers and necklaces made from Job's tears over our heads, as my four adult children and the other members of our party walked between these rows of people.

Two people carried the banner ahead of us and then a singing group from the village of Mbanzing led us to the center of the village, where six or seven hundred people gathered. The dancers were dressed in traditional garb and wore elegant headdresses, extending three feet into the air.

They played drums, singing Christian words to a traditional song. At the center of the village green, the dancers changed from the traditional style of movement to form the shape of a large cross. Then the dance leader, Manape, reverently danced alongside the others as if outlining the shape of the cross.

When he came back to the base of the cross formation, he stopped. Then he lifted his feather headdress, reverently placed it on the ground at the foot of the cross and knelt. His head touched the ground, his hands stretched ahead of him.

Then each one of the dancers took off his elaborate headdress and bowed to the ground before the crucified Christ. It was an absolutely electrifying moment of worship for them and for us.

The day continued with unique skits, a variety of dances and kind hospitality. The next day Miliŋnâŋe's sister, a sweet old lady, came to me and led me to the other side of the village. I knew that various groups planned more dramas. I could hear a group practicing songs off to one side. My first thought, when Miliŋnâŋe's sister asked me to come with her, was that they maybe wanted me to come on stage at the appropriate time, representing the coming of the white missionary in one of their skits.

But no, instead, all the women from the Sanau clan were there, each dressed in traditional string skirts. They presented me with new string skirts, and dressed me, putting one on top of the other. They fussed over me, tying the skirts just so.

When I asked what I had to do they said, "Aw, you only have to shake hands." They smiled and looked at each other with knowing looks. "We'll tell you when," they added. I went back and sat down.

Soon members of the Sanau clan gathered in a semi-circle in the village green. Miliŋnâŋe's widow, Mutalac, called me to come before her. She began, "We as a community have never said sorry for killing Edmund." A hush fell over the crowd as she spoke these words to me in the Nabak language. "It was my husband who killed your husband. I say it out plainly that we killed Fabian. I have been in your home and you have been in mine. We have hiked together on the trail, but whenever you and I meet I feel like there is a barrier between us. I don't feel comfortable; I feel guilty," she said.

My eyes brimmed with tears as she continued, "We have cried because of this and you have cried. We have been angry about what happened and I'm sure you have been angry. Now you are a widow and I too am a widow.

"But from today we don't want to cry any more. We want to be happy because God's Talk has come to us. Now instead of crying and feeling guilty I have a question to ask you."

"What is it?" I asked.

"Would you, would you consider being my sister?"

The question caught me off guard. I remembered that my first Nabak name was "White Person." Then one day when bandaging a tropical ulcer someone called me "White Woman." Then I moved up in society to be "Fourth born." But "Sister?" That had nothing to do with the color of my skin, my gender or my birth order. This would be family. She wanted to call me, "My Sister."

I said, "Yes, it would be an honor to be your sister."

Then she gave me a beautiful heirloom piece, called 'the side of a pig'. It is made up of a large quantity of dogs' teeth filed down and carefully sewn onto a mat. This important article is placed on top of a butchered pig and given as part of the bride price payment to the brother of the bride. This particular item had been given to Miliŋnâŋe at the marriage of his sister many years previously.

I was deeply touched by this present that in their social structure represented not only wealth, but shrewdness in hunting and trading. They would have exchanged one of the sharp teeth of a certain opossum that lives in their jungle for fifty dogs' teeth.

It was not enough for Mutalac to say "sorry". Social relationships among the Nabaks are not held together by words but require visible and concrete expression. This wealth item would symbolize the social bonding which she was beginning with me at that moment.

Then she led me around the semi-circle of relatives. To her first-born daughter standing at her side she said, "This is your aunt." Then she turned to me, "Let me introduce you to your niece." Maiwe, my new niece, and I hugged and cried together. She also gave me a gift.

Mutalac took me around to each one in that circle. Oh, they were people I already knew, but now I paused before each one as she gave me the kin term by which I should address each of them. "This is your cousin. This is your uncle. This is your older brother..." In this tear-filled ritual I was lovingly inducted into the Sanau family. I shook hands or hugged each one. We cried together. They presented me with beautiful artifacts.

Then one after the other each of my four children, starting with Jonathan, was called out from the audience and led around this same semi-circle. "Let me introduce you to your grandfather. This is your older sister..." They were hugged, just as I had been, and given priceless family heirlooms in different designs, boar's tusks, garden produce and net bags.

My sister and brother-in-law came to Papua New Guinea for the Nabak New Testament celebrations. It was only appropriate to include them in the ceremonies and lavish them with many special gifts.

Nothing was hurried but everything proceeded according to Nabak protocol with heart-felt dignity. The ceremony closed when the village leader had us move from our semi-circle formation to a long line. We joined elbows in a people chain, facing the crowd. "I now introduce you to the new Sanau clan," he said to them.

All the struggles with learning the language, our successes and failures in the project, the malaria, the computer problems, the misunderstandings, everything came together and distilled in a moment so full of emotion I thought I would burst.

I have pondered that extraordinary experience many times since that eventful day. I remember how eager and full of dedication Edmund and I were when we first arrived in Papua New Guinea. We came to show God's love but they also showed us glimpses of God's love. We came to teach them. But they were the ones to demonstrate to us a superb model of the process of reconciliation. I came thinking I had given up my parents and family, only to find that I was given new relationships that have enriched my life beyond the telling. I thought nothing could be more beautiful than seeing the newly printed Nabak New Testaments coming out from under that red cloth and being dedicated to the glory of God, and then I saw not only the books, but the truth of one of the central themes of Scripture walk right out of its pages and that was the absolute high point of the festivities.

I could only say, "Lord, You did this. You have triumphed gloriously. The powers of darkness have been pushed back. Bravo, Lord, bravo!"

Dietlinde accepting the family heirlooms from Miliŋnâŋe's wife Mutalac during the Nabak reconciliation ceremony. "This is your new sister. This is your new aunt…"

❧ CHAPTER THIRTY-EIGHT

The book stays

> *""The gospel is like a caged lion.*
> *It does not need to be defended,*
> *it just needs to be*
> *let out of the cage."* [71]

My heart bubbled up in praise to God through those days of celebration. The Nabak people had very lovingly and carefully planned every detail. I was told, "Since you did most of the work on the translation, you can rest and enjoy the week. We will do all the work for the dedication." Their only request was that I give one speech.

What should I say? How could I put a lifetime of experiences into a fifteen or twenty minute speech? I prayed. I agonized. Out of a heart of love, I spoke these words to the Nabak people that weekend.

"When we came to Kasanombe in 1969, I was a young woman carrying a new baby in my arms. Now look at me. What do you see—a young woman or an old woman? I have white hair and all of my children are grown men and women. Now I have grandchildren.

"Why did I stay here so long with you? Each of you think about it.

"Some of my time among you was fun—like learning to work alongside of you in your gardens. You tried to teach me to make a

---

net bag but my hand was heavy and we all laughed together. We had lots of good times together, didn't we?

"But it was not only that. Some of the time among you was difficult—like when we first came and Gwakâp's wife bled to death and we were helpless to do anything. Then we were attacked by criminals in Lae. They stoned our house and were going to kill us.

"Then there was the time we had to leave the Bumayong Settlement and move to Ukarumpa. A very big sorrow hit us in 1987 when Kondo died. Then more recently Edmund died and that was an extraordinarily sad time.

"Why did I stay even when faced with these heartaches, sickness and death? I will tell you clearly that there were two reasons.

"One reason was that God said to me, "Grace, don't leave. I want you to stay, in spite of the troubles. I am with you. I will help you. Stay and give the Nabak people my words."

"And so I stayed, even though your language is complicated and I was sick with malaria, even though I was very scared sometimes.

"The second reason I didn't leave is because I have come to love you. I am very fond of you. I taught some of you to read. I delivered your babies. You told me your stories and taught me your songs. I have prayed every day for you. Even when hard times came, I couldn't leave you. I feel deeply for you.

"But let me tell you something that is even more special. This book, in your very own language, tells you that God loves you. That's amazing, isn't it? I had to stay until you had this wonderful book in your hands and could read for yourselves that God loves you.

"Now I want to say thank you. Thank you for letting us live in your village, and for being patient when we made mistakes. Thank you for teaching us to sing your incredible songs, for sharing your food. Thank you for carrying my cargo on the trail, and for stopping to rest when I couldn't take another step. Thank you for giving me the privilege of delivering your babies and bandaging your sores. Thank you for sitting with me and rubbing my sore hand. Thank you for crying with me.

"If it would be possible, and of course it isn't, to go back and become a young woman again, I would choose to do the same thing—to live among you and translate the Bible for you because I love you and because I want you to read God's love letter to you.

"I beg you to buy and read God's Word. Buy it for your children and grandchildren. Teach them to read it. They need to know that God loves them too. Of all the messages that could be shouted over the mountains, this is the most important message they could ever hear.

"Now I will close with an adaptation of Paul's words to the Ephesian Christians in Acts 20. You know how I lived the whole time I was with you, from the first day I came into Papua New Guinea. I served the Lord with great humility and with tears. You know that I have not hesitated to preach anything that would be helpful to you but have taught you publicly and from house to house. I have declared to all that they must turn to God in repentance and have faith in our Lord Jesus. I consider my life worth nothing to me, if only I may finish the race and complete the task the Lord Jesus has give me—the task of testifying to the gospel of God's grace. I have not hesitated to proclaim to you the whole will of God.

"Keep watch over yourselves and all the flock of which the Holy Spirit has made you overseers. Be shepherds of the church of God that He bought with His own blood. I know that after I leave, false teachers will come in among you and will not spare the flock. Even from your own number men may arise and distort the truth in order to draw away disciples after them. So be on your guard. Remember that for twenty-nine years I never stopped warning each of you night and day with tears.

"Now I commit you to God and to the word of His grace, which can build you up and give you an inheritance among all those who are sanctified."

I was pretty choked up as I spoke. My eyes had always been set on this goal of finishing the Nabak translation. Now with that goal reached, I had to consider the possibility that I wouldn't always be here for them, or they for me. Some day I might have to leave my adopted country and my Nabak family, but I wasn't abandoning them. My comfort was that the book would stay. The Bible, after all, is the best missionary.

This book had guided and sustained me. Now its grace-filled words in their own Nabak language could direct and strengthen them. God's amazing grace can help them rise above the difficulties. He was there for me and I know He wouldn't fail them either.

He couldn't.

God's outrageous grace would be enough.

Epilogue

Digging away in my backyard, I am reminded that just like I have a plan for my garden, so God is working out His eternal purposes in my life. The rose bushes I planted when I moved to Pennsylvania in 2005 have produced beautifully. I believe that with all the digging, losses and disturbances in our lives God is up to something we can't imagine. He knows better than we. In His hands He turns our losses into beautiful flowers.

Roses were Edmund's favorite flower. A rose is engraved on his headstone in Papua New Guinea, and I think of him as I water these bushes in my garden. Their vibrant red petals add beauty and fragrance that wasn't here before, just like God added a new perspective, a gentleness into my life that couldn't have been there before Edmund died. Sometimes it feels that the tragedy happened just yesterday, but Edmund gave his life for what he loved. I can be sad for myself but how can I be sad about that?

I bend to smell one of the roses, cupped in my hand, and remember Kondo smelling the roses outside the translation office. What truth he spoke. We cannot know God's love if we cannot smell His fragrance. What an honor God gave me, to bring the fragrance of Jesus to my friends, the Nabak people.

Since the dedication of the Nabak New Testament, Zumbek gained more skills in translation principles and became a translation consultant. He traveled to Israel and studied Hebrew at Jerusalem University with the goal of translating the Old Testament into Nabak. His wife Egue died of ovarian cancer shortly after he returned to Papua New Guinea. In the last moments of her life she sat up in bed, reached her arms heavenward and said, "Jesus, oh, Jesus." Then fell back on the bed and passed into glory. Zumbek feels the loss keenly. Pray for him and the three children.

Others on the translation team continue in literacy work and Scripture distribution. I know of some who have received teacher training, and Martin has developed a very creative method of teaching reading through singing Nabak hymns.

The original hymn book is sold out, so I am hoping at some point to return to Papua New Guinea for a brief visit, to revise the hymn book and collect any new songs they might have written since then. The Nabaks love to sing and this will be a great companion volume to their New Testament.

The last time I saw Mutalac, my Nabak sister, was when we visited her village to hold a writers' workshop. She rushed out to the airstrip to meet me, then led me to her house. Before being inducted into the Sanau clan, I would have stayed in the home of a village leader, but now as part of the Sanau family I stayed in Mutalac's home and she took care of me. I miss her very much.

On the 15th anniversary of their father's death, as a symbol of their growth in God's love, I planted a fruit tree for each one of my children. What a joy they are to me.

My oldest, Jonathan, and his wife Amy are blessed with six beautiful children. They live close to me now, which allows me to see them often, and each of them is growing up with this story as a special part of their family's history. Even now, Jonathan has reconnected with the way the Lord moved in him after his father's death, bringing him closer to God.

Dietlinde has completed her master's degree in education, and has spent years teaching children in Indonesia and Africa. She burns with a desire to lift up children in poverty; her compassion is powerful indeed. She is working towards a long-term goal of starting a school for children in poverty in Africa.

My youngest daughter Heidi has spent years in India, teaching street children who have no one else to care about them. She has learned the difficult language of Hindi, and has seen some of "her kids" grow from boys into young men. She faces risks each day, but her gentleness and patience have served well to keep her safe.

Kurt, Heidi's twin brother, has recently completed a masters degree program in Clinical Psychology, and now uses those skills to help people heal from emotional damage. We have long talks about theology and psychology, and he wonders if he won't go some place around the world to use his talents some day.

My own journey didn't end with Edmund's death, or with the dedication of the New Testament. Since the celebrations, I journeyed a short time longer with the Nabaks and then returned to the U.S.A. to be with my own father for his 97-99th years of life. In 2002, I returned to Papua New Guinea, but in a new capacity, to teach at Christian Leaders' Training College. Teaching God's Word, writing workbooks, and pouring my life's experiences into the lives of eager young men and women was a delightful icing-on-the-cake experience.

I left Papua New Guinea in 2005, but my ministry here is fruitful and flourishing. I now reside in Pennsylvania to be close to my sons and am blessed to have my own house. I speak, teach and write, hoping that others will be inspired to join in the work of reaching Bibleless people groups.

What God did for me, my family and among the Nabak people is all because of His grace. I am only a minor player. And what He does now and continues to do as the translation committee works on the Nabak Old Testament, the Nabak hymnbook and literacy projects is still His outrageous grace.

I have learned that giving God's Word to a people group is something worth dying for. It is something worth living for. And I have learned that He did not fail me. And dear reader, I can say with full confidence that when He gives you a task that demands radical obedience, He won't fail you either. Because God has written the script, and because His outrageous grace flows over us, we can turn the pages to a new chapter. There CAN be music again.

Lord, may music and love flow out from our lives.
Equip us, by the presence of your Holy Spirit,
for a powerful performance.

The Fabian family in 1978.

Upper Left to Right: Heidi, Edmund, Grace, Kurt
Lower Left to Right: Jonathan and Dietlinde

The Fabian family today.

Upper Left to Right: Jonathan, Isaiah (J's 2nd), Heidi, Amy (J's wife), Isaac (J's 1st)
Lower Left to Right: Dietlinde, Grace holding Elijah(J's 6th), Ian (J's 4th), Leah (J's 3rd), Ethan (J's 5th), Kurt

For more details check out

www.GraceFabian.com

- Chapter by chapter study guide questions
- Many more pictures
- Movie clips of Nabak people and dedication
- Monthly devotionals
- Details about the story not in the book
- Learn how Grace can speak to your group
- Contact Grace directly

Read about Grace's Story in:

The Covering
Author: Hank Hanegraaff
Publisher: Thomas Nelson

In His Everlasting Arms: Learning to Trust God in All Circumstances
Author: Gail MacDonald
Publisher: Vine Books

Light
Author: Mark Winheld
Publisher: Brundage Publishing